Bake Sale TODAY!

Cookies 25¢

Cupcakes 50¢

R.Q.Daly

CLASSIC Bake Sale

R E C I P E S

PiL
Publications International, Ltd.

Microwave Cooking: Microwave ovens vary in wattage. Use the cooking times as guidelines and check for doneness before adding more time.

Preparation/Cooking Times: Preparation times are based on the approximate amount of time required to assemble the recipe before cooking, baking, chilling or serving. These times include preparation steps such as measuring, chopping and mixing. The fact that some preparations and cooking can be done simultaneously is taken into account. Preparation of optional ingredients and serving suggestions are not included.

Table of Contents

Introduction 6

Cookies by the Dozen 10

Unbelievable Bar Cookies 30

Blockbuster Brownies 50

Quick Breads and Muffins 68

Luscious Cakes 86

Blue-Ribbon Pies 108

Acknowledgments 122

Index 123

Technique

The basis of a successful bake sale is quality baked goods. Use of the following techniques will guarantee perfect results every time.

- Read the entire recipe before beginning to be sure you have all the necessary ingredients and utensils.
- Remove butter, margarine and cream cheese from the refrigerator to soften, if necessary.
- Measure all the ingredients accurately and assemble them in the order they are listed in the recipe.
- Use the pan size specified in the recipe. Prepare the pans according to the recipe directions.
- Adjust oven racks and preheat the oven. Check oven temperature for accuracy with an oven thermometer.
- Follow recipe directions and baking times exactly. Check for doneness using the test given in the recipe.
- To measure dry ingredients, always use standardized measuring spoons and cups. Fill the appropriate measuring spoon or cup to overflowing and level it off with a metal spatula or flat edge of a knife.
- To measure liquid ingredients, use a standardized glass or plastic measuring cup with a pouring spout. Place the cup on a flat surface, fill to the desired mark and check the measurement at eye level.

Decorating

The success of a bake sale depends not only on the quality of the treats, but also on their appearance. Small touches can make the difference between left over and sold out. Use these easy tips to add a professional touch to your baked goods.

- Partially or completely dip cookies in melted chocolate and place on waxed paper until the chocolate is set.

• Use a spoon or fork to drizzle chocolate over the tops of cookies, bars, cakes or breads.

• Add a dusting of powdered sugar or cocoa powder to your baked goods. Spoon the sugar or cocoa into a sieve and gently tap the side to send down a flurry of goodness. Don't sprinkle too far in advance or the powdered sugar may dissolve and disappear.

• Drizzle fudge, caramel or butterscotch ice cream toppings over your baked goods.

• Decorate cookies, bars and cupcakes with colored sugar or sprinkles.

Packaging

Decide whether your baked goods will be sold whole or by the piece.

When selling them whole or as a bunch, use plastic wrap or cellophane to wrap cookies, breads and pies. Then tie with ribbons or raffia. Cookies can be stacked and tied together with cord or sold in decorative boxes or bags.

If your baked goods will be sold individually, it's a good idea to wrap each piece in plastic wrap or cellophane. Then place them on a colorful platter or pile them in a basket lined with colorful napkins. If you decide not to wrap them, provide tongs so people can serve themselves without touching the treats.

Storage and Freezing

Be ready for an unexpected bake sale by baking and freezing items ahead of time. Many unbaked doughs can be prepared in advance and frozen. Then just a few minutes in the oven create a fresh-baked treat. Use the following guidelines for your make-ahead goodies. No matter what you are freezing, remember to label it with the recipe name and date.

Cookies & Bars

Unbaked cookie dough can be refrigerated for up to one week or frozen for up to six months. Rolls of dough (for slice-and-bake cookies) should be sealed tightly in plastic wrap; other doughs should be stored in airtight containers. Label the container with baking information for convenience. When ready to use, thaw dough at room temperature 15 to 30 minutes. Freeze baked cookies in airtight containers or freezer bags for up to six months. Crisp cookies freeze better than soft, moist cookies. Rich, buttery bar cookies freeze extremely well. Thaw, unwrapped, at room temperature.

After baking, store soft and crisp cookies separately at room temperature to protect against changes in texture and flavor. Soft cookies should be stored in airtight containers. Crisp cookies are best stored in containers with loose-fitting lids to prevent moisture buildup. Store cookies with sticky glazes or fragile decorations in single layers between sheets of waxed paper.

Breads and Muffins

Quick breads should be wrapped well in plastic wrap and stored at room temperature for up to three days or wrapped in heavy-duty foil and frozen for up to three months. Muffins should be stored in a sealed plastic food storage bag for up to three days or frozen for up to one month wrapped in heavy-duty foil.

Cakes

Do not freeze cakes with cream or fruit fillings. Unfrosted cakes can be frozen for up to 4 months; thaw, unwrapped, at room temperature.

Frosted cakes should be frozen unwrapped until the frosting hardens. Then wrap, seal and freeze for up to two months. To thaw, remove wrapping and thaw at room temperature or in the refrigerator. Refrigerate cakes with whipped cream frostings or cream fillings.

Store one-layer cakes in their baking pans, tightly covered. Store layer cakes in a cake-saver or under a large inverted bowl.

Pies

Unbaked pie dough can be frozen for later use. Flatten the dough into circles and stack them in a freezer bag with waxed paper between each layer. Thaw dough before rolling it out and placing it in a pie pan.

To freeze unbaked pies, do not cut steam vents in the top crust. Cover with an inverted paper plate for extra protection and wrap with plastic wrap or place in a freezer bag. To bake, do not thaw. Cut slits in top crust and allow additional 15 to 20 minutes of baking time.

Baked pies can also be cooled and frozen. To serve, let the pie thaw at room temperature for two hours, then heat until warm. Pies with cream or custard fillings and toppings do not freeze well.

Do not freeze meringue-topped pies. They are best when served the day they are made; leftovers should be refrigerated. Custard or cream pies should be refrigerated immediately after cooling. Fruit pies should be covered and stored at room temperature overnight; refrigerate for longer storage.

Cookies by the Dozen

No other treat is as versatile as the cookie—dainty sugar cookies, hearty raisin-studded oatmeal cookies or rich chocolate cookies. This chapter has cookies perfect for any occasion.

Soft Apple Cider Cookies

    1 cup firmly packed light brown sugar
    $^{1}/_{2}$ cup FLEISCHMANN'S® Original Margarine, softened
    $^{1}/_{2}$ cup apple cider
    $^{1}/_{2}$ cup EGG BEATERS® Healthy Real Egg Product
    2 $^{1}/_{4}$ cups all-purpose flour
    1 $^{1}/_{2}$ teaspoons ground cinnamon
    1 teaspoon baking soda
    $^{1}/_{4}$ teaspoon salt
    2 medium apples, peeled and diced (about 1 $^{1}/_{2}$ cups)
    $^{3}/_{4}$ cup almonds, chopped
    Cider Glaze (recipe follows)

In large bowl, with electric mixer at medium speed, beat sugar and
margarine until creamy. Add cider and Egg Beaters®; beat until smooth.
With electric mixer at low speed, gradually blend in flour, cinnamon,
baking soda and salt. Stir in apples and almonds.

Drop dough by tablespoonfuls, 2 inches apart, onto greased baking sheets.
Bake at 375°F for 10 to 12 minutes or until golden brown. Remove
from sheets; cool on wire racks. Drizzle with Cider Glaze.

Makes 4 dozen cookies

Cider Glaze: In small bowl, combine 1 cup powdered sugar and
2 tablespoons apple cider until smooth.

Prep Time: 30 minutes
Bake Time: 12 minutes

Chocolate Chip Sandwich Cookies

COOKIES

1 package DUNCAN HINES® Chocolate Chip Cookie Mix
1 egg
$^1/_3$ cup vegetable oil
3 tablespoons water

CREAM FILLING

$1^1/_2$ cups marshmallow creme
$^3/_4$ cup butter or margarine, softened
$2^1/_2$ cups powdered sugar
$1^1/_2$ teaspoons vanilla extract

1. Preheat oven to 375°F.

2. **For Cookies,** combine cookie mix, egg, oil and water in large bowl. Stir until thoroughly blended. Drop by rounded teaspoonfuls 2 inches apart onto ungreased cookie sheets. Bake at 375°F for 8 to 10 minutes or until light golden brown. Cool 1 minute on cookie sheets. Remove to wire racks.

3. **For Cream Filling,** combine marshmallow creme and butter in large bowl. Add powdered sugar and vanilla extract, beating until smooth.

4. To assemble, spread bottoms of half the cookies with 1 tablespoon cream filling; top with remaining cookies. Press together to make sandwich cookies. Refrigerate to quickly firm the filling, if desired.

Makes about 24 sandwich cookies

Tip: After chilling the assembled cookies, wrap individually in plastic wrap. Store in the refrigerator until ready to serve.

Chocolate Chip Sandwich Cookies

Honey Ginger Snaps

        2 cups all-purpose flour
        1 tablespoon ground ginger
        2 teaspoons baking soda
    $^{1}/_{8}$ teaspoon salt
    $^{1}/_{8}$ teaspoon ground cloves
    $^{1}/_{2}$ cup shortening
    $^{1}/_{4}$ cup butter, softened
    1$^{1}/_{2}$ cups sugar, divided
    $^{1}/_{4}$ cup honey
        1 egg
        1 teaspoon vanilla

Preheat oven to 350°F. Grease cookie sheets. Combine flour, ginger, baking soda, salt and cloves in medium bowl.

Beat shortening and butter in large bowl with electric mixer at medium speed until smooth. Gradually beat in 1 cup sugar until blended; increase speed to high and beat until light and fluffy. Beat in honey, egg and vanilla until fluffy. Gradually stir in flour mixture until blended.

Shape mixture into 1-inch balls. Place remaining $^{1}/_{2}$ cup sugar in shallow bowl; roll balls in sugar to coat. Place 2 inches apart on prepared cookie sheets.

Bake 10 minutes or until golden brown. Let cookies stand on cookie sheets 5 minutes; transfer to wire racks to cool completely. Store in airtight container up to 1 week. *Makes 3$^{1}/_{2}$ dozen cookies*

Honey Ginger Snaps

Mexican Wedding Cookies

1 cup pecan pieces or halves
1 cup butter, softened
2 cups powdered sugar, divided
2 cups all-purpose flour, divided
2 teaspoons vanilla
$1/8$ teaspoon salt

Place pecans in food processor. Process using on/off pulsing action until pecans are ground, but not pasty.

Beat butter and $1/2$ cup powdered sugar in large bowl with electric mixer at medium speed until light and fluffy. Gradually add 1 cup flour, vanilla and salt. Beat at low speed until well blended. Stir in remaining 1 cup flour and ground nuts with spoon.

Shape dough into ball; wrap in plastic wrap and refrigerate 1 hour or until firm.

Preheat oven to 350°F. Shape tablespoons of dough into 1-inch balls. Place 1 inch apart on ungreased cookie sheets.

Bake 12 to 15 minutes or until pale golden brown. Let cookies stand on cookie sheets 2 minutes.

Meanwhile, place 1 cup powdered sugar in 13×9-inch glass dish. Transfer hot cookies to powdered sugar. Roll cookies in powdered sugar, coating well. Let cookies cool in sugar.

Sift remaining $1/2$ cup powdered sugar over sugar-coated cookies before serving. Store tightly covered at room temperature or freeze up to 1 month.   *Makes about 4 dozen cookies*

Easy Lemon Cookies

1 package DUNCAN HINES® Moist Deluxe Lemon Cake Mix
2 eggs
¹/₂ cup vegetable oil
1 teaspoon grated lemon peel
Pecan halves, for garnish

1. Preheat oven to 350°F.

2. Combine cake mix, eggs, oil and lemon peel in large bowl. Stir until thoroughly blended. Drop by rounded teaspoonfuls 2 inches apart onto ungreased cookie sheets. Press pecan half in center of each cookie. Bake at 350°F for 9 to 11 minutes or until edges are light golden brown. Cool 1 minute on cookie sheets. Remove to wire racks. Cool completely. Store in airtight container.   *Makes 4 dozen cookies*

Tip: You may substitute whole almonds or walnut halves for the pecan halves.

Be sure to wash lemons with warm, soapy water to
remove wax and traces of insecticide before grating
the peel.

Toffee Chunk Brownie Cookies

    1 cup butter
    4 ounces unsweetened chocolate, coarsely chopped
1 1/2 cups sugar
    2 eggs
    1 tablespoon vanilla
    3 cups all-purpose flour
  1/8 teaspoon salt
1 1/2 cups coarsely chopped chocolate-covered toffee bars

Preheat oven to 350°F. Melt butter and chocolate in large saucepan over low heat, stirring until smooth. Remove from heat; cool slightly.

Stir sugar into chocolate mixture until smooth. Stir in eggs until well blended. Stir in vanilla until smooth. Stir in flour and salt just until mixed. Fold in chopped toffee.

Drop heaping tablespoonfuls of dough 1 1/2 inches apart onto *ungreased* cookie sheets.

Bake 12 minutes or until just set. Let cookies stand on cookie sheets 5 minutes; transfer to wire racks to cool completely. Store in airtight container.   *Makes 36 cookies*

*Allow cookie sheets to cool between batches; the
dough will spread if it is placed on a hot cookie sheet.*

Toffee Chunk Brownie Cookies

Marbled Biscotti

$^1/_2$ cup (1 stick) butter or margarine, softened

1 cup granulated sugar

2 large eggs

1 teaspoon vanilla extract

$2^1/_2$ cups all-purpose flour

1 teaspoon baking powder

1 teaspoon baking soda

$1^3/_4$ cups "M&M's"® Chocolate Mini Baking Bits, divided

1 cup slivered almonds, toasted*

$^1/_4$ cup unsweetened cocoa powder

2 tablespoons instant coffee granules

*To toast almonds, spread in single layer on baking sheet. Bake at 350°F for 7 to 10 minutes until light golden, stirring occasionally. Remove almonds from pan and cool completely before using.

Preheat oven to 350°F. Lightly grease cookie sheets; set aside. In large bowl cream butter and sugar until light and fluffy; beat in eggs and vanilla. In medium bowl combine flour, baking powder and baking soda; blend into creamed mixture. Dough will be stiff. Stir in $1^1/_4$ cups "M&M's"® Chocolate Mini Baking Bits and nuts. Divide dough in half. Add cocoa powder and coffee granules to half of the dough, mixing to blend. On well-floured surface, gently knead doughs together just enough to marble. Divide dough in half and gently roll each half into 12×2-inch log; place on prepared cookie sheets at least 4 inches apart. Press remaining $^1/_2$ cup "M&M's"® Chocolate Mini Baking Bits onto outside of both logs. Bake 25 minutes. Dough will spread. Cool logs 15 to 20 minutes. Slice each log into 12 slices; arrange on cookie sheet cut-side down. Bake an additional 10 minutes. (For softer biscotti, omit second baking.) Cool completely. Store in tightly covered container. *Makes 24 pieces*

Marbled Biscotti

Peanut Butter Chocolate Chippers

    1 cup creamy or chunky peanut butter
    1 cup firmly packed light brown sugar
    1 large egg
    3/4 cup milk chocolate chips
        Granulated sugar

1. Preheat oven to 350°F.

2. Combine peanut butter, sugar and egg in medium bowl; mix with mixing spoon until well blended. Add chips; mix well.

3. Roll heaping tablespoonfuls of dough into 1 1/2-inch balls. Place balls 2 inches apart on ungreased cookie sheets.

4. Dip table fork into granulated sugar; press criss-cross fashion onto each ball, flattening to 1/2-inch thickness.

5. Bake 12 minutes or until set. Let cookies stand on cookie sheets 2 minutes. Remove cookies with spatula to wire racks; cool completely.

Makes about 2 dozen cookies

Note: This simple recipe is unusual because it doesn't contain any flour—but it still makes great cookies.

Shiny, heavy-gauge aluminum baking sheets promote even browning of cookies; dark sheets absorb more heat, causing cookies to brown too quickly. Reduce oven temperature by 25°F when using dark sheets.

Peanut Butter Chocolate Chippers

Refrigerator Cookies

$^1/_2$ cup sugar

$^1/_4$ cup light corn syrup

$^1/_4$ cup margarine, softened

$^1/_4$ cup cholesterol-free egg substitute

1 teaspoon vanilla

1 $^3/_4$ cups all-purpose flour

$^1/_4$ teaspoon baking soda

$^1/_4$ teaspoon salt

Cookie decorations (optional)

1. Beat sugar, corn syrup and margarine in large bowl. Add egg substitute and vanilla; mix well. Set aside.

2. Combine flour, baking soda and salt in medium bowl. Add to sugar mixture; mix well. Form dough into 2 (1$^1/_2$-inch-wide) rolls. Wrap in plastic wrap. Freeze 1 hour.

3. Preheat oven to 350°F. Cover baking sheets with parchment paper. Cut dough into $^1/_4$-inch-thick slices; place 1 inch apart on prepared cookie sheets. Sprinkle with cookie decorations, if desired.

4. Bake 8 to 10 minutes or until edges begin to turn golden brown. Cool on wire racks.   *Makes about 4 dozen cookies*

Variation: Add 2 tablespoons unsweetened cocoa powder to dough for chocolate cookies.

Refrigerator Cookies

Peanut Gems

2^1/$_2$ cups all-purpose flour
1 teaspoon baking powder
^{1}/$_8$ teaspoon salt
1 cup butter, softened
1 cup packed light brown sugar
2 eggs
2 teaspoons vanilla
1^1/$_2$ cups cocktail peanuts, finely chopped
Powdered sugar (optional)

Preheat oven to 350°F. Combine flour, baking powder and salt in small bowl.

Beat butter in large bowl with electric mixer at medium speed until smooth. Gradually beat in brown sugar; increase speed to medium-high and beat until light and fluffy. Beat in eggs, 1 at a time, until fluffy. Beat in vanilla. Gradually stir in flour mixture until blended. Stir in peanuts until blended.

Drop heaping tablespoonfuls of dough about 1 inch apart onto ungreased cookie sheets; flatten slightly with hands.

Bake 12 minutes or until set. Let cookies stand on cookie sheets 5 minutes; transfer to wire racks to cool completely. Dust cookies with powdered sugar, if desired. Store in airtight container.

Makes 2^1/$_2$ dozen cookies

Oatmeal Raisin Cookies

3/4 cup all-purpose flour

3/4 teaspoon salt

1/2 teaspoon baking soda

1/2 teaspoon ground cinnamon

3/4 cup butter, softened

3/4 cup granulated sugar

3/4 cup packed light brown sugar

1 egg

1 tablespoon water

3 teaspoons vanilla, divided

3 cups uncooked quick-cooking or old-fashioned oats

1 cup raisins

1/2 cup powdered sugar

1 tablespoon milk

Preheat oven to 375°F. Grease cookie sheets; set aside. Combine flour, salt, baking soda and cinnamon in small bowl.

Beat butter, granulated sugar and brown sugar in large bowl with electric mixer at medium speed until light and fluffy. Add egg, water and 2 teaspoons vanilla; beat well. Add flour mixture; beat at low speed just until blended. Stir in oats with spoon. Stir in raisins.

Drop tablespoonfuls of dough 2 inches apart onto prepared cookie sheets.

Bake 10 to 11 minutes or until edges are golden brown. Let cookies stand 2 minutes on cookie sheets; transfer to wire racks to cool completely.

For glaze, stir powdered sugar, milk and remaining 1 teaspoon vanilla in small bowl until smooth. Drizzle over cookies. Store tightly covered at room temperature.

Makes about 4 dozen cookies

Choco-Caramel Delights

$^{1}/_{2}$ cup (1 stick) butter or margarine, softened

$^{2}/_{3}$ cup sugar

1 egg, separated

2 tablespoons milk

1 teaspoon vanilla extract

1 cup all-purpose flour

$^{1}/_{3}$ cup HERSHEY'S Cocoa

$^{1}/_{4}$ teaspoon salt

1 cup finely chopped pecans

Caramel Filling (recipe follows)

$^{1}/_{2}$ cup HERSHEY'S Semi-Sweet Chocolate Chips

1 teaspoon shortening (do not use butter, margarine, spread or oil)

1. Beat butter, sugar, egg yolk, milk and vanilla in medium bowl until blended. Stir together flour, cocoa and salt; blend into butter mixture. Refrigerate dough at least 1 hour or until firm enough to handle.

2. Heat oven to 350°F. Lightly grease cookie sheet.

3. Beat egg white slightly. Shape dough into 1-inch balls. Dip each ball into egg white; roll in pecans to coat. Place on prepared cookie sheet. Press thumb gently in center of each ball. Bake 10 to 12 minutes or until set.

4. Meanwhile, prepare Caramel Filling. Remove cookies from oven; press center of each cookie again with thumb to make indentation. Immediately spoon about $^{1}/_{2}$ teaspoon Caramel Filling in center of each cookie. Carefully remove from cookie sheets; cool on wire racks.

5. Place chocolate chips and shortening in small microwave-safe bowl. Microwave at HIGH (100%) 1 minute or until softened; stir. Allow to stand several minutes to finish melting; stir until smooth. Place wax paper under wire rack with cookies. Drizzle chocolate mixture over tops of cookies.

Makes about 2 dozen cookies

Caramel Filling: In small saucepan, combine 14 unwrapped light caramels and 3 tablespoons whipping cream. Cook over low heat, stirring frequently, until caramels are melted and mixture is smooth.

Choco-Caramel Delights

Unbelievable Bar Cookies

*Quick to prepare, quick to disappear!
These rich bar-cookie recipes whip up in
no time—great for last-minute events.*

Naomi's Revel Bars

1 cup plus 2 tablespoons butter, softened and divided
2 cups packed brown sugar
2 eggs
2 teaspoons vanilla
2½ cups all-purpose flour
1 teaspoon baking soda
3 cups uncooked old-fashioned or quick oats
1 package (12 ounces) semisweet chocolate chips
1 can (14 ounces) sweetened condensed milk

Preheat oven to 325°F. Lightly grease 13×9-inch baking pan.

Beat 1 cup butter and sugar in large bowl with electric mixer until light and fluffy. Add eggs; beat until blended. Stir in vanilla.

Combine flour and baking soda in medium bowl; stir into butter mixture. Stir in oats. Spread ¾ of oat mixture evenly in prepared pan.

Combine chocolate chips, milk and remaining 2 tablespoons butter in small heavy saucepan. Stir over low heat until chocolate is melted. Pour chocolate mixture evenly over oat mixture in pan. Dot with remaining oat mixture.

Bake 20 to 25 minutes or until edges are browned and center feels firm. Cool in pan on wire rack. Cut into bars. *Makes about 3 dozen bars*

Choco-Lowfat Strawberry Shortbread Bars

$^1/_4$ cup ($^1/_2$ stick) corn oil spread (60% oil)

$^1/_2$ cup sugar

1 egg white

$1^1/_4$ cups all-purpose flour

$^1/_4$ cup HERSHEY'S Cocoa or HERSHEY'S Dutch Processed Cocoa

$^3/_4$ teaspoon cream of tartar

$^1/_2$ teaspoon baking soda

Dash salt

$^1/_2$ cup strawberry all-fruit spread

White Chip Drizzle (recipe follows)

Heat oven to 375°F. Lightly spray 13×9×2-inch baking pan with vegetable cooking spray.

Combine corn oil spread and sugar in medium bowl; beat on medium speed of electric mixer until well blended. Add egg white; beat until well blended. Stir together flour, cocoa, cream of tartar, baking soda and salt; gradually add to sugar mixture, beating well. Gently press mixture onto bottom of prepared pan.

Bake 10 to 12 minutes or just until set. Cool completely in pan on wire rack. Spread fruit spread evenly over crust. Cut into bars or other desired shapes with cookie cutters. Prepare White Chip Drizzle; drizzle over tops of bars. Let stand until set. *Makes 3 dozen bars*

White Chip Drizzle

¹/₃ cup HERSHEY₀S Premier White Chips
¹/₂ teaspoon shortening (do not use butter, margarine, spread or oil)

Place white chips and shortening in small microwave-safe bowl. Microwave at HIGH (100% power) 30 seconds; stir. If necessary, microwave at HIGH an additional 15 seconds at a time, stirring after each heating, just until chips are melted when stirred. Use immediately.

Choco-Lowfat Strawberry Shortbread Bars

Luscious Lemon Bars

2 cups all-purpose flour

1 cup butter

$^1/_2$ cup powdered sugar

4 teaspoons grated lemon peel, divided

$^1/_4$ teaspoon salt

1 cup granulated sugar

3 large eggs

$^1/_3$ cup fresh lemon juice

Sifted powdered sugar

1. Preheat oven to 350°F. Grease 13×9-inch baking pan; set aside. Place flour, butter, powdered sugar, 1 teaspoon lemon peel and salt in food processor. Process until mixture forms coarse crumbs.

2. Press mixture evenly into prepared baking pan. Bake 18 to 20 minutes or until golden brown.

3. Beat granulated sugar, eggs, lemon juice and remaining 3 teaspoons lemon peel in medium bowl with electric mixer at medium speed until well blended.

4. Pour mixture evenly over warm crust. Return to oven; bake 18 to 20 minutes or until center is set and edges are golden brown. Remove pan to wire rack; cool completely.

5. Dust with sifted powdered sugar; cut into 2×1$^1/_2$-inch bars.

6. Store tightly covered at room temperature. *Do not freeze.*

Makes 3 dozen bars

Luscious Lemon Bars

Chocolate Caramel Pecan Bars

 2 cups butter, softened and divided
 $^1/_2$ cup granulated sugar, divided
 1 egg
 $2^3/_4$ cups all-purpose flour
 $^2/_3$ cup packed light brown sugar
 $^1/_4$ cup light corn syrup
 $2^1/_2$ cups coarsely chopped pecans
 1 cup semisweet chocolate chips

1. Preheat oven to 375°F. Grease 15×10-inch jelly-roll pan; set aside.

2. Beat 1 cup butter and granulated sugar in large bowl with electric mixer at medium speed until light and fluffy. Beat in egg. Add flour. Beat at low speed until just blended. Spread dough into prepared pan. Bake 20 minutes or until light golden brown.

3. Meanwhile, prepare topping. Combine remaining 1 cup butter, brown sugar and corn syrup in medium heavy saucepan. Bring to a boil over medium heat, stirring frequently. Boil 2 minutes without stirring. Quickly stir in pecans; spread over base. Bake 20 minutes or until dark golden brown and bubbling.

4. Immediately sprinkle chocolate chips evenly over hot caramel. Gently press chips into caramel topping with spatula. Loosen caramel from edges of pan with spatula or knife. Cool completely in pan on wire rack. Cut into 3×1$^1/_2$-inch bars. Store tightly covered at room temperature or freeze up to 3 months. *Makes 40 bars*

Chocolate Caramel Pecan Bars

Chocolate Orange Gems

²/₃ cup butter-flavored solid vegetable shortening

³/₄ cup firmly packed light brown sugar

1 large egg

¹/₄ cup orange juice

1 tablespoon grated orange zest

2¹/₄ cups all-purpose flour

¹/₂ teaspoon baking powder

¹/₂ teaspoon baking soda

¹/₂ teaspoon salt

1³/₄ cups "M&M's"® Chocolate Mini Baking Bits

1 cup coarsely chopped pecans

¹/₃ cup orange marmalade

Vanilla Glaze (recipe follows)

Preheat oven to 350°F. In large bowl cream shortening and sugar until light and fluffy; beat in egg, orange juice and orange zest. In medium bowl combine flour, baking powder, baking soda and salt; blend into creamed mixture. Stir in "M&M's"® Chocolate Mini Baking Bits and nuts. Reserve 1 cup dough; spread remaining dough into ungreased 13×9×2-inch baking pan. Spread marmalade evenly over top of dough to within ¹/₂ inch of edges. Drop reserved dough by teaspoonfuls randomly over marmalade. Bake 25 to 30 minutes or until light golden brown. *Do not overbake.* Cool completely; drizzle with Vanilla Glaze. Cut into bars. Store in tightly covered container. *Makes 2 dozen bars*

Vanilla Glaze: Combine 1 cup powdered sugar and 1 to 1$\frac{1}{2}$ tablespoons warm water until desired consistency. Place glaze in resealable plastic sandwich bag; seal bag. Cut a tiny piece off one corner of the bag (not more than $\frac{1}{8}$ inch). Drizzle glaze over cookies.

Chocolate Orange Gems

Strawberry Oat Bars

1 cup butter, softened
1 cup firmly packed light brown sugar
2 cups uncooked quick oats
1 cup all-purpose flour
2 teaspoons baking soda
1/2 teaspoon ground cinnamon
1/4 teaspoon salt
1 can (21 ounces) strawberry pie filling
3/4 teaspoon almond extract

Preheat oven to 375°F. Beat butter in large bowl with electric mixer at medium speed until smooth. Add brown sugar; beat until well blended.

Combine oats, flour, baking soda, cinnamon and salt in large bowl; mix well. Add flour mixture to butter mixture, beating on low speed until well blended and crumbly.

Spread 2/3 of crumb mixture in bottom of ungreased 13×9-inch baking pan, pressing to form firm layer. Bake 15 minutes; let cool 5 minutes on wire rack.

Meanwhile, place strawberry filling in food processor or blender; process until smooth. Stir in almond extract.

Pour strawberry mixture over partially baked crust. Sprinkle remaining crumb mixture evenly over strawberry layer.

Return pan to oven; bake 20 to 25 minutes or until topping is golden brown and filling is slightly bubbly. Let cool completely on wire rack before cutting into bars. *Makes about 4 dozen bars*

Strawberry Oat Bars

Chocolate Chip Cookie Bars

1 1/4 cups firmly packed light brown sugar

3/4 Butter Flavor* CRISCO® Stick or 3/4 cup Butter Flavor* CRISCO® all-vegetable shortening plus additional for greasing

2 tablespoons milk

1 tablespoon vanilla

1 egg

1 3/4 cups all-purpose flour

1 teaspoon salt

3/4 teaspoon baking soda

1 cup (6 ounces) semisweet chocolate chips

1 cup coarsely chopped pecans** (optional)

*Butter Flavor Crisco is artificially flavored.

**If pecans are omitted, add an additional 1/2 cup semisweet chocolate chips.

1. Heat oven to 350°F. Grease 13×9-inch baking pan. Place cooling rack on countertop.

2. Place brown sugar, shortening, milk and vanilla in large bowl. Beat at medium speed of electric mixer until well blended. Add egg; beat well.

3. Combine flour, salt and baking soda. Add to shortening mixture; beat at low speed just until blended. Stir in chocolate chips and pecans, if desired.

4. Press dough evenly onto bottom of prepared pan.

5. Bake at 350°F for 20 to 25 minutes or until lightly browned and firm in the center. *Do not overbake.* Cool completely on cooling rack. Cut into 2×1 1/2-inch bars.   *Makes about 3 dozen bars*

Chocolate Chip Cookie Bars

Pecan Pie Bars

$^3/_4$ cup butter

$^1/_2$ cup powdered sugar

$1^1/_2$ cups all-purpose flour

3 eggs

2 cups coarsely chopped pecans

1 cup granulated sugar

1 cup light corn syrup

2 tablespoons butter, melted

1 teaspoon vanilla

Preheat oven to 350°F. For crust, beat butter in large bowl with electric mixer at medium speed until smooth. Add powdered sugar; beat at medium speed until well blended.

Add flour gradually, beating at low speed after each addition. (Mixture will be crumbly but presses together easily.)

Press dough evenly into ungreased 13×9-inch baking pan. Press mixture slightly up sides of pan (less than $^1/_4$ inch) to form lip to hold filling.

Bake 20 to 25 minutes or until golden brown. Meanwhile, for filling, beat eggs lightly in medium bowl with fork. Add pecans, granulated sugar, corn syrup, melted butter and vanilla; mix well.

Pour filling over partially baked crust. Return to oven; bake 35 to 40 minutes or until filling is set.

Loosen edges with knife. Let cool completely on wire rack before cutting into squares. Cover and refrigerate until 10 to 15 minutes before serving time. *Do not freeze.*   *Makes about 4 dozen bars*

Cherry Butterscotch Bars

2 cups plus 1 tablespoon all-purpose flour, divided

3/4 cup firmly packed brown sugar

3/4 cup butter, softened

2 eggs

1/4 cup butterscotch chips, melted

1 teaspoon baking powder

1 teaspoon vanilla

1/4 teaspoon salt

1/2 cup chopped maraschino cherries, drained

1/2 cup butterscotch chips

Maraschino cherries

Butterscotch chips

Powdered sugar

1. Preheat oven to 350°F. Grease and flour 13×9-inch baking pan.

2. Combine 2 cups flour, brown sugar, butter, eggs, 1/4 cup melted chips, baking powder, vanilla and salt in large bowl. Beat at low speed of electric mixer, scraping bowl often, until well mixed, 1 to 2 minutes.

3. Mix chopped cherries and remaining 1 tablespoon flour in small bowl. Stir cherries and 1/2 cup chips into butter mixture. Spread batter in prepared pan.

4. Bake 25 to 35 minutes or until edges are lightly browned. Cool completely. Sprinkle with additional cherries, chips and powdered sugar. Cut into bars.

Makes about 3 dozen bars

Currant Cheesecake Bars

$^1/_2$ cup butter, softened

1 cup all-purpose flour

$^1/_2$ cup packed light brown sugar

$^1/_2$ cup finely chopped pecans

1 package (8 ounces) cream cheese, softened

$^1/_4$ cup granulated sugar

1 egg

1 tablespoon milk

2 teaspoons grated lemon peel

$^1/_3$ cup currant jelly or seedless raspberry jam

Preheat oven to 350°F. Grease 9-inch square baking pan. Beat butter in medium bowl with electric mixer at medium speed until smooth. Add flour, brown sugar and pecans; beat at low speed until well blended. Press mixture into bottom and partially up sides of prepared pan. Bake about 15 minutes or until light brown. If sides of crust have shrunk down, press back up and reshape with spoon. Let cool 5 minutes on wire rack.

Meanwhile, beat cream cheese in large bowl with electric mixer at medium speed until smooth. Add granulated sugar, egg, milk and lemon peel; beat until well blended.

Heat jelly in small saucepan over low heat 2 to 3 minutes or until smooth, stirring occasionally. Pour cream cheese mixture over crust. Drizzle jelly in 7 to 8 horizontal strips across filling with spoon. Swirl jelly through filling with knife to create marbled effect.

Bake 20 to 25 minutes or until filling is set. Cool completely on wire rack before cutting into bars. Store in airtight container in refrigerator up to 1 week. *Makes about 32 bars*

Currant Cheesecake Bars

Mystical Layered Bars

$^1/_3$ cup butter or margarine

1 cup graham cracker crumbs

$^1/_2$ cup uncooked old-fashioned or quick oats

1 can (14 ounces) sweetened condensed milk

1 cup flaked coconut

$^3/_4$ cup semisweet chocolate chips

$^3/_4$ cup raisins

1 cup coarsely chopped pecans

Preheat oven to 350°F. Melt butter in 13×9-inch baking pan. Remove from oven.

Sprinkle graham cracker crumbs and oats evenly over margarine; press with fork. Drizzle condensed milk over oats. Layer coconut, chocolate chips, raisins and pecans over milk.

Bake 25 to 30 minutes or until lightly browned. Cool in pan on wire rack 5 minutes; cut into 2×1$^1/_2$-inch bars. Cool completely in pan on wire rack. Store tightly covered at room temperature or freeze up to 3 months.

Makes 3 dozen bars

Marshmallow Krispie Bars

1 package DUNCAN HINES® Chewy Fudge Brownie Mix

1 package (10$^1/_2$ ounces) miniature marshmallows

1$^1/_2$ cups semi-sweet chocolate chips

1 cup creamy peanut butter

1 tablespoon butter or margarine

1$^1/_2$ cups crisp rice cereal

1. Preheat oven to 350°F. Grease bottom of 13×9-inch pan.

2. Prepare and bake brownies following package directions for cake-like recipe. Remove from oven. Sprinkle marshmallows on hot brownies. Return to oven. Bake for 3 minutes longer.

3. Place chocolate chips, peanut butter and butter in medium saucepan. Cook over low heat, stirring constantly, until chips are melted. Add rice cereal; mix well. Spread mixture over marshmallow layer. Refrigerate until chilled. Cut into bars. *Makes about 2 dozen bars*

Tip: For a special presentation, cut cookies into diamond shapes.

To soften raisins that have become extremely hard during storage, place ¹/₂ cup of raisins in a 1-cup microwavable bowl. Cover with water and heat at HIGH 2 to 2¹/₂ minutes. Allow to stand 3 to 5 minutes; drain.

Blockbuster Brownies

Who can resist a dense chocolatey piece of heaven? Whether you like your brownies frosted or plain, fudgy or cakelike, you're sure to find the perfect match for your cravings.

Rocky Road Brownies

$^{1}/_{2}$ cup butter

$^{1}/_{2}$ cup unsweetened cocoa

1 cup sugar

$^{1}/_{2}$ cup all-purpose flour

$^{1}/_{4}$ cup buttermilk

1 egg

1 teaspoon vanilla

1 cup miniature marshmallows

1 cup coarsely chopped walnuts

1 cup (6 ounces) semisweet chocolate chips

Preheat oven to 350°F. Lightly grease 8-inch square pan. Combine butter and cocoa in medium saucepan over low heat, stirring constantly until smooth. Remove from heat; stir in sugar, flour, buttermilk, egg and vanilla. Mix until smooth. Spread batter evenly in prepared pan. Bake 25 minutes or until center feels dry. (Do not overbake or brownies will be dry.) Remove from oven; sprinkle with marshmallows, walnuts and chocolate chips. Return to oven for 3 to 5 minutes or just until topping is warmed enough to meld. Cool in pan on wire rack. Cut into 2-inch squares.

Makes 16 brownies

When baking brownies, always use the size of pan called for in the recipe. Using a smaller pan will result in brownies that are undercooked and gummy in the middle. Brownies will be dry and thin if baked in a larger pan.

Double "Topped" Brownies

BROWNIES

    1 package DUNCAN HINES® Chocolate Lovers Double Fudge
       Brownie Mix

    2 eggs

    1/3 cup water

    1/4 cup vegetable oil plus additional for greasing

    1/2 cup flaked coconut

    1/2 cup chopped nuts

FROSTING

    3 cups confectioners' sugar

    1/3 cup shortening

  1 1/2 teaspoons vanilla extract

    2 to 3 tablespoons milk

TOPPING

    3 squares (3 ounces) unsweetened chocolate

    1 tablespoon butter or margarine

1. Preheat oven to 350°F. Grease bottom of 13×9-inch pan.

2. For brownies, combine brownie mix, fudge packet from mix, eggs, water and oil in large bowl. Stir with spoon until well blended, about 50 strokes. Stir in coconut and nuts. Spread in prepared pan. Bake at 350°F for 27 to 30 minutes or until set. Cool completely.

3. For frosting, combine confectioners' sugar, shortening and vanilla extract. Stir in milk, 1 tablespoon at a time, until frosting is of spreading consistency. Spread over cooled brownies. Refrigerate until frosting is firm, about 30 minutes.

4. For topping, melt chocolate and butter in small bowl over hot water; stir until smooth. Drizzle over frosting. Refrigerate until chocolate is firm, about 15 minutes. Cut into bars.   *Makes about 4 dozen brownies*

Double "Topped" Brownies

Marbled Peanut Butter Brownies

$^{1}/_{2}$ cup butter, softened

$^{1}/_{4}$ cup peanut butter

1 cup packed light brown sugar

$^{1}/_{2}$ cup granulated sugar

3 eggs

1 teaspoon vanilla

2 cups all-purpose flour

2 teaspoons baking powder

$^{1}/_{8}$ teaspoon salt

1 cup chocolate-flavored syrup

$^{1}/_{2}$ cup coarsely chopped salted mixed nuts

Preheat oven to 350°F. Lightly grease 13×9-inch pan. Beat butter and peanut butter in large bowl until blended; stir in sugars. Beat in eggs, one at a time, until batter is light. Blend in vanilla. Combine flour, baking powder and salt in small bowl. Stir into butter mixture. Spread half of the batter evenly into prepared pan. Spread syrup over top. Spoon remaining batter over syrup. Swirl with knife or spatula to create marbled effect. Sprinkle with chopped nuts. Bake 35 to 40 minutes or until lightly browned. Cool in pan on wire rack. Cut into 2-inch squares.

Makes about 2 dozen brownies

*Baking powder can lose its leavening ability
if stored improperly or kept too long. Check the
"use by" date stamped on the container before
purchasing. Store baking powder in a cool, dry place. Use
within six months of opening.*

Marbled Peanut Butter Brownies

Mini Brownie Cups

$^1/_4$ cup ($^1/_2$ stick) (56 to 60% corn oil) spread

2 egg whites

1 egg

$^3/_4$ cup sugar

$^2/_3$ cup all-purpose flour

$^1/_3$ cup HERSHEY'S Cocoa

$^1/_2$ teaspoon baking powder

$^1/_4$ teaspoon salt

Mocha Glaze (recipe follows)

Heat oven to 350°F. Line small muffin cups ($1^3/_4$ inches in diameter) with paper bake cups or spray with vegetable cooking spray.

Melt corn oil spread in small saucepan over low heat; cool slightly. Beat egg whites and egg in small mixer bowl, on medium speed of electric mixer, until foamy; gradually add sugar, beating until slightly thickened and light in color. Stir together flour, cocoa, baking powder and salt; gradually add to egg mixture, beating until blended. Gradually add corn oil spread, beating just until blended. Fill muffin cups $^2/_3$ full with batter.

Bake 15 to 18 minutes or until wooden pick inserted in center comes out clean. Remove from pan to wire rack. Cool completely. Prepare Mocha Glaze; drizzle over tops of brownie cups. Let stand until glaze is set.

Makes 2 dozen servings

Mocha Glaze

- $^1/_4$ **cup powdered sugar**
- $^3/_4$ **teaspoon HERSHEY'S Cocoa**
- $^1/_4$ **teaspoon powdered instant coffee**
- 2 **teaspoons hot water**
- $^1/_4$ **teaspoon vanilla extract**

Stir together powdered sugar and cocoa in small bowl. Dissolve coffee in water; gradually add to sugar mixture, stirring until well blended. Stir in vanilla.

Mini Brownie Cups

Minted Chocolate Chip Brownies

3/4 cup granulated sugar

1/2 cup butter

2 tablespoons water

1 cup semisweet chocolate chips or mini semisweet chocolate
   chips

1 1/2 teaspoons vanilla

2 eggs

1 1/4 cups all-purpose flour

1/2 teaspoon baking soda

1/2 teaspoon salt

1 cup mint chocolate chips

Powdered sugar for garnish

Preheat oven to 350°F. Grease 9-inch square baking pan. Combine sugar, butter and water in medium microwavable bowl. Microwave on HIGH 2 1/2 to 3 minutes or until butter is melted. Stir in semisweet chips; stir gently until chips are melted and mixture is well blended. Stir in vanilla; let stand 5 minutes to cool.

Beat eggs into chocolate mixture, one at a time. Combine flour, baking soda and salt in small bowl; add to chocolate mixture. Stir in mint chocolate chips. Spread into prepared pan.

Bake 25 minutes for fudgy brownies or 30 minutes for cakelike brownies.

Remove pan to wire rack; cool completely. Cut into 2 1/4-inch squares. Sprinkle with powdered sugar, if desired.   *Makes about 16 brownies*

Minted Chocolate Chip Brownies

Baker's® One Bowl® Brownies

4 squares BAKER'S® Unsweetened Baking Chocolate

¾ cup (1½ sticks) butter *or* margarine

2 cups sugar

3 eggs

1 teaspoon vanilla

1 cup flour

1 cup coarsely chopped nuts (optional)

White Chocolate Glaze, optional (recipe follows)

HEAT oven to 350°F (325°F for glass baking dish). Line 13×9-inch baking pan with foil extending over edges to form handles. Grease foil.

MICROWAVE chocolate and butter in large microwavable bowl on HIGH 2 minutes or until butter is melted. Stir until chocolate is completely melted.

STIR sugar into chocolate until well blended. Mix in eggs and vanilla. Stir in flour and nuts until well blended. Spread in prepared pan.

BAKE 30 to 35 minutes or until toothpick inserted into center comes out with fudgy crumbs. *Do not overbake.* Cool in pan. Lift out of pan onto cutting board. Cut into squares.   *Makes 2 dozen fudgy brownies*

White Chocolate Glaze: Microwave ⅓ cup heavy whipping cream in medium microwavable bowl on HIGH for 45 seconds or until simmering. Add 1 package (6 squares) Baker's® Premium White Baking Chocolate, finely chopped. Stir until white chocolate is melted and mixture is smooth.

Prep Time: 15 minutes
Bake Time: 35 minutes

Baker's® One Bowl® Brownies

Caramel Fudge Brownies

1 jar (12 ounces) hot caramel ice cream topping
1 1/4 cups all-purpose flour, divided
1/4 teaspoon baking powder
    Dash salt
4 squares (1 ounce each) unsweetened chocolate, coarsely chopped
3/4 cup butter
2 cups sugar
3 eggs
2 teaspoons vanilla
3/4 cup semisweet chocolate chips
3/4 cup chopped pecans

1. Preheat oven to 350°F. Lightly grease 13×9-inch baking pan.

2. Combine caramel topping and 1/4 cup flour in small bowl; set aside.

3. Combine remaining 1 cup flour, baking powder and salt in small bowl; mix well.

4. Place unsweetened chocolate squares and butter in medium microwavable bowl. Microwave at HIGH 2 minutes or until butter is melted; stir until chocolate is completely melted.

5. Stir sugar into melted chocolate. Add eggs and vanilla; stir until combined.

6. Add flour mixture, stirring until well blended. Spread chocolate mixture evenly into prepared pan.

7. Bake 25 minutes. Immediately after removing brownies from oven, spread caramel mixture over brownies. Sprinkle top evenly with chocolate chips and pecans.

8. Return pan to oven; bake 20 to 25 minutes or until topping is golden brown and bubbling. *Do not overbake.* Cool brownies completely in pan on wire rack. Cut into 2×1 1/2-inch bars.

9. Store tightly covered at room temperature or freeze up to 3 months.

Makes 3 dozen brownies

Butterscotch Brownies

    1 cup butterscotch-flavored chips
    1/4 cup butter, softened
    1/2 cup packed light brown sugar
    2 eggs
    1/2 teaspoon vanilla
    1 cup all-purpose flour
    1/2 teaspoon baking powder
    1/4 teaspoon salt
    1 cup semisweet chocolate chips

Preheat oven to 350°F. Grease 9-inch square baking pan. Melt butterscotch chips in small saucepan over low heat, stirring constantly; set aside.

Beat butter and sugar in large bowl until light and fluffy. Beat in eggs, one at a time. Beat in melted butterscotch chips and vanilla. Combine flour, baking powder and salt in small bowl; add to butter mixture. Beat until well blended. Spread batter evenly into prepared pan.

Bake 20 to 25 minutes or until golden brown and center is set. Remove pan from oven and immediately sprinkle with chocolate chips. Let stand about 4 minutes or until chocolate is melted. Spread chocolate evenly over top. Place pan on wire rack; cool completely. Cut into 2 1/4-inch squares.

Makes about 16 brownies

Fabulous Blonde Brownies

1¾ cups all-purpose flour

1 teaspoon baking powder

¼ teaspoon salt

1 cup (6 ounces) white chocolate chips

1 cup (4 ounces) blanched whole almonds, coarsely chopped

1 cup English toffee bits

⅔ cup butter, softened

1½ cups packed light brown sugar

2 eggs

2 teaspoons vanilla

Preheat oven to 350°F. Lightly grease 13×9-inch baking pan.

Combine flour, baking powder and salt in small bowl; mix well. Combine white chocolate, almonds and toffee in medium bowl; mix well.

Beat butter and brown sugar in large bowl with electric mixer at medium speed until light and fluffy. Beat in eggs and vanilla. Add flour mixture; beat at low speed until well blended. Stir in ¾ cup of white chocolate mixture. Spread evenly into prepared pan.

Bake 20 minutes. Immediately after removing brownies from oven, sprinkle remaining white chocolate mixture evenly over brownies. Press lightly. Bake 15 to 20 minutes or until wooden pick inserted into center comes out clean. Cool brownies completely in pan on wire rack. Cut into 2×1½-inch bars. *Makes 3 dozen brownies*

Fabulous Blonde Brownies

Quick & Easy Fudgey Brownies

4 bars (1 ounce each) HERSHEY'S Unsweetened Baking
    Chocolate, broken into pieces
³/₄ cup (1¹/₂ sticks) butter or margarine
2 cups sugar
3 eggs
1¹/₂ teaspoons vanilla extract
1 cup all-purpose flour
1 cup chopped nuts (optional)
Creamy Quick Chocolate Frosting (recipe follows, optional)

Heat oven to 350°F. Grease 13×9×2-inch baking pan.

Place chocolate and butter in large microwave-safe bowl. Microwave at
HIGH 1¹/₂ to 2 minutes or until chocolate is melted and mixture is
smooth when stirred. Add sugar; stir with spoon until well blended. Add
eggs and vanilla; mix well. Add flour and nuts, if desired; stir until well
blended. Spread into prepared pan.

Bake 30 to 35 minutes or until wooden pick inserted in center comes out
almost clean. Cool in pan on wire rack.

Frost with Creamy Quick Chocolate Frosting, if desired. Cut into squares.

Makes about 2 dozen brownies

Creamy Quick Chocolate Frosting

3 tablespoons butter or margarine
3 bars (1 ounce each) HERSHEY'S Unsweetened Baking
    Chocolate, broken into pieces
3 cups powdered sugar
$^1/_2$ cup milk
1 teaspoon vanilla extract
$^1/_8$ teaspoon salt

Melt butter and chocolate in saucepan over very low heat. Cook, stirring constantly, until chocolate is melted and mixture is smooth. Pour into large bowl; add powdered sugar, milk, vanilla and salt. Beat on medium speed of electric mixer until well blended. If necessary, refrigerate 10 minutes or until of spreading consistency.   *Makes about 2 cups frosting*

Quick & Easy Fudgey Brownies

Quick Breads and Muffins

With this variety of moist, tender quick breads, you are sure to please everyone. Thank goodness they're so easy—you'll need to make plenty!

Walnut-Chocolate Quick Bread

1 1/2 cups milk

1 cup sugar

1/3 cup vegetable oil

1 egg, beaten

1 tablespoon molasses

1 teaspoon vanilla

3 cups all-purpose flour

3 tablespoons unsweetened cocoa powder

2 teaspoons baking soda

2 teaspoons baking powder

1 teaspoon salt

1 cup chocolate chips

1/2 cup walnuts, coarsely chopped

1. Preheat oven to 350°F. Grease four 5×3-inch loaf pans; set aside.

2. Combine milk, sugar, oil, egg, molasses and vanilla in medium bowl. Stir until sugar is dissolved; set aside.

3. Whisk together flour, cocoa, baking soda, baking powder and salt in large bowl. Add chocolate chips, nuts and sugar mixture; stir just until combined. Pour into prepared pans.

4. Bake 30 minutes or until toothpick inserted near center of loaf comes out clean. Cool in pan 15 minutes. Remove from pan and cool on wire rack.

Makes 4 loaves

Muffin Variation: Preheat oven to 375°F. Spoon batter into 12 greased muffin cups. Bake 20 minutes or until toothpick inserted near center of muffin comes out clean. Makes 12 muffins.

Apple Butter Spice Muffins

$^1/_2$ cup sugar

1 teaspoon ground cinnamon

$^1/_4$ teaspoon ground nutmeg

$^1/_8$ teaspoon ground allspice

$^1/_2$ cup pecans or walnuts, chopped

2 cups all-purpose flour

2 teaspoons baking powder

$^1/_4$ teaspoon salt

1 cup milk

$^1/_4$ cup vegetable oil

1 egg

$^1/_4$ cup apple butter

1. Preheat oven to 400°F. Grease or paper-line 12 (2$^1/_2$-inch) muffin cups.

2. Combine sugar, cinnamon, nutmeg and allspice in large bowl. Toss 2 tablespoons sugar mixture with pecans in small bowl; set aside. Add flour, baking powder and salt to remaining sugar mixture.

3. Combine milk, oil and egg in medium bowl. Stir into flour mixture just until moistened.

4. Spoon 1 tablespoon batter into each prepared muffin cup. Spoon 1 teaspoon apple butter into each cup. Spoon remaining batter evenly over apple butter. Sprinkle reserved pecan mixture over each muffin. Bake 20 to 25 minutes or until golden brown and wooden toothpick inserted in center comes out clean. Immediately remove from pan; cool on wire rack 10 minutes. Serve warm or cold. *Makes 12 muffins*

Apple Butter Spice Muffins

Brunch-Time Zucchini-Date Bread

BREAD

    1 cup chopped pitted dates

    1 cup water

    1 cup whole wheat flour

    1 cup all-purpose flour

    2 tablespoons sugar

    1 teaspoon baking powder

    $1/2$ teaspoon baking soda

    $1/2$ teaspoon salt

    $1/2$ teaspoon ground cinnamon

    $1/4$ teaspoon ground cloves

    2 eggs

    1 cup shredded zucchini, pressed dry with paper towels

CREAM CHEESE SPREAD

    1 package (8 ounces) reduced-fat cream cheese

    $1/4$ cup powdered sugar

    1 tablespoon vanilla

    $1/8$ teaspoon ground cinnamon

    Dash ground cloves

1. Preheat oven to 350°F. Spray 8×4×2-inch loaf pan with nonstick cooking spray.

2. Combine dates and water in small saucepan. Bring to a boil over medium-high heat. Remove from heat; let stand 15 minutes.

3. Combine flours, sugar, baking powder, baking soda, salt, cinnamon and cloves in large bowl. Beat eggs in medium bowl; stir in date mixture and zucchini. Stir egg mixture into flour mixture just until dry ingredients are moistened. Pour batter evenly into prepared pan.

4. Bake 30 to 35 minutes or until toothpick inserted into center comes out clean. Cool 5 minutes. Remove from pan. Cool completely on wire rack.

5. Meanwhile, to prepare cream cheese spread, combine cream cheese, sugar, vanilla, cinnamon and cloves in small bowl. Beat until smooth. Cover and refrigerate until ready to use.

6. Cut bread into 16 slices. Serve with cream cheese spread.

Makes 16 servings

*It is important not to overmix quick bread batter.
After the combined wet ingredients are added
to the combined dry ingredients, mix only until the
mixture is evenly moistened. The batter should look
lumpy when it goes into the prepared pan.
Too much stirring or beating will give the bread a
tough texture with lots of holes and tunnels.*

Baker's® Chocolate Chunk Sour Cream Muffins

$^1/_2$ cup milk

2 tablespoons MAXWELL HOUSE® Instant Coffee, any variety

$1^1/_2$ cups flour

$^1/_2$ cup sugar

$1^1/_2$ teaspoons CALUMET® Baking Powder

$^1/_2$ teaspoon cinnamon

$^1/_4$ teaspoon salt

2 eggs

$^1/_2$ cup BREAKSTONE'S® Sour Cream *or* plain yogurt

$^1/_4$ cup ($^1/_2$ stick) butter *or* margarine, melted

1 teaspoon vanilla

1 package (4 ounces) BAKER'S® GERMAN'S® Sweet Baking Chocolate, chopped

HEAT oven to 375°F.

STIR milk and instant coffee in small bowl until well blended; set aside. Mix flour, sugar, baking powder, cinnamon and salt in large bowl. Beat eggs in small bowl; stir in coffee-milk mixture, sour cream, butter and vanilla until well blended. Add flour mixture; stir just until moistened. Stir in chopped chocolate.

SPOON batter into greased or paper-lined muffin pan, filling each cup $^2/_3$ full.

BAKE for 30 minutes or until toothpick inserted into center comes out clean. Serve warm. *Makes 12 muffins*

Prep Time: 15 minutes
Bake Time: 30 minutes

Baker's® Chocolate Chunk Sour Cream Muffins and Baker's® Chocolate Chunk Banana Bread (page 80)

Cranberry Poppy Seed Loaf

2^{1}/$_{2}$ cups all-purpose flour

^{3}/$_{4}$ cup granulated sugar

2 tablespoons poppy seeds

1 tablespoon baking powder

1 cup fat-free (skim) milk

^{1}/$_{3}$ cup FLEISCHMANN'S® Original Margarine, melted

^{1}/$_{4}$ cup EGG BEATERS® Healthy Real Egg Product

1 teaspoon vanilla extract

2 teaspoons grated lemon peel

1 cup fresh or frozen cranberries, chopped

Powdered Sugar Glaze, optional (recipe follows)

In large bowl, combine flour, granulated sugar, poppy seeds and baking powder; set aside.

In small bowl, combine milk, margarine, Egg Beaters®, vanilla and lemon peel. Stir milk mixture into flour mixture just until moistened. Stir in cranberries. Spread batter into greased 8^{1}/$_{2}$×4^{1}/$_{2}$×2^{1}/$_{4}$-inch loaf pan. Bake at 350°F for 60 to 70 minutes or until toothpick inserted in center comes out clean. Cool in pan on wire rack. Drizzle with Powdered Sugar Glaze, if desired. *Makes 12 servings*

Powdered Sugar Glaze: In small bowl, combine 1 cup powdered sugar and 5 to 6 teaspoons water until smooth.

Cranberry Poppy Seed Loaf

Applesauce-Spice Bread

1 1/2 cups all-purpose flour
1 cup unsweetened applesauce
3/4 cup packed light brown sugar
1/4 cup shortening
1 egg
1 teaspoon vanilla
3/4 teaspoon baking soda
3/4 teaspoon ground cinnamon
1/4 teaspoon baking powder
1/4 teaspoon salt
1/4 teaspoon ground nutmeg
1/2 cup toasted chopped walnuts
1/2 cup raisins (optional)
    Powdered sugar

Preheat oven to 350°F. Spray 9-inch square baking pan with nonstick cooking spray; set aside.

Beat flour, applesauce, brown sugar, shortening, egg, vanilla, baking soda, cinnamon, baking powder, salt and nutmeg in large bowl with electric mixer at low speed 30 seconds. Increase speed to high; beat 3 minutes. Stir in walnuts and raisins, if desired. Pour into prepared pan.

Bake 30 minutes or until brown and toothpick inserted into center comes out clean. Cool in pan on wire rack. Sprinkle with powdered sugar.

Makes 9 servings

Applesauce-Spice Bread

Baker's® Chocolate Chunk Banana Bread

2 eggs, lightly beaten
1 cup mashed ripe bananas
1/3 cup oil
1/4 cup milk
2 cups flour
1 cup sugar
2 teaspoons CALUMET® Baking Powder
1/4 teaspoon salt
1 package (4 ounces) BAKER'S® GERMAN'S® Sweet Baking Chocolate, coarsely chopped
1/2 cup chopped nuts

HEAT oven to 350°F.

STIR eggs, bananas, oil and milk until well blended. Add flour, sugar, baking powder and salt; stir until just moistened. Stir in chocolate and nuts. Pour into greased 9×5-inch loaf pan.

BAKE for 55 minutes or until toothpick inserted into center comes out clean. Cool in pan 10 minutes. Remove from pan; cool completely on wire rack.   *Makes 18 (1/2-inch) servings*

Note: For easier slicing, wrap bread and store overnight.

Prep Time: 15 minutes
Bake Time: 55 minutes

Gingerbread Pear Muffins

1 ¾ cups all-purpose flour

⅓ cup sugar

2 teaspoons baking powder

¾ teaspoon ground ginger

¼ teaspoon baking soda

¼ teaspoon salt

¼ teaspoon ground cinnamon

⅓ cup milk

¼ cup vegetable oil

¼ cup light molasses

1 egg

1 medium pear, peeled, cored and finely chopped

1. Preheat oven to 375°F. Grease or paper-line 12 (2½-inch) muffin cups.

2. Sift flour, sugar, baking powder, ginger, baking soda, salt and cinnamon into large bowl.

3. Combine milk, oil, molasses and egg in medium bowl. Stir in pear. Stir milk mixture into flour mixture just until moistened.

4. Spoon evenly into prepared muffin cups, filling two-thirds full.

5. Bake 20 minutes or until wooden toothpick inserted into centers comes out clean. Immediately remove from pan; cool on wire rack 10 minutes. Serve warm or cold.

Makes 12 muffins

Nutmeg Strawberry Muffins

2 cups stemmed and halved (quartered if large) California
strawberries (about 1 pint basket)
2 cups plus 1 tablespoon sugar, divided
$^1/_2$ cup plus 1 tablespoon cornmeal, divided
3$^1/_4$ teaspoons nutmeg, divided
3 cups flour
1 teaspoon salt
1 teaspoon baking soda
1$^1/_4$ cups vegetable oil
4 eggs, beaten
1 cup chopped walnuts

Preheat oven to 375°F. Toss strawberries with 1 tablespoon sugar in medium bowl; set aside. Combine 1 tablespoon sugar, 1 tablespoon cornmeal and $^1/_4$ teaspoon nutmeg for topping; set aside. Combine flour, remaining sugar, $^1/_2$ cup cornmeal, 3 teaspoons nutmeg, salt and baking soda in large bowl. Add oil and eggs to strawberry mixture; mix gently. Add strawberry mixture and walnuts to flour mixture; mix just until dry ingredients are moistened. Measure $^1/_3$ cup batter into 24 paper-lined or greased 2$^3/_4$-inch muffin cups. Sprinkle reserved topping mixture over muffins. Bake in center of oven about 25 minutes or until springy to the touch and wooden toothpick inserted into centers comes out clean. Cooled muffins can be frozen up to 2 months. *Makes 24 muffins*

Nutmeg Strawberry Bread: Prepare batter as directed above. Pour into two greased 8×4-inch loaf pans; sprinkle loaves with topping mixture. Bake in preheated 375°F oven about 1 hour and 10 minutes or until toothpick inserted into centers comes out clean. Cool on rack.

Favorite recipe from **California Strawberry Commission**

Nutmeg Strawberry Muffins

Orange Cinnamon Swirl Bread

BREAD

    1 package DUNCAN HINES® Cinnamon Swirl Muffin Mix

    1 egg

$2/3$ cup orange juice

    1 tablespoon grated orange peel

ORANGE GLAZE

    $1/2$ cup confectioners' sugar

    2 to 3 teaspoons orange juice

    1 teaspoon grated orange peel

    Quartered orange slices, for garnish (optional)

1. Preheat oven to 350°F. Grease and flour $8^{1}/_{2} \times 4^{1}/_{2} \times 2^{1}/_{2}$-inch loaf pan.

2. For bread, combine muffin mix and contents of topping packet from mix in large bowl. Break up any lumps. Add egg, $2/3$ cup orange juice and 1 tablespoon orange peel. Stir until moistened, about 50 strokes. Knead swirl packet from mix for 10 seconds before opening. Squeeze contents on top of batter. Swirl into batter with knife or spatula, folding from bottom of bowl to get an even swirl. *Do not completely mix in.* Pour into pan. Bake at 350°F 55 to 60 minutes or until toothpick inserted in center comes out clean. Cool in pan 10 minutes. Loosen loaf from pan. Invert onto cooling rack. Turn right side up. Cool completely.

3. For orange glaze, place confectioners' sugar in small bowl. Add orange juice, 1 teaspoon at a time, stirring until smooth and desired consistency. Stir in 1 teaspoon orange peel. Drizzle over loaf. Garnish with orange slices, if desired.

Makes 1 loaf (12 slices)

Tip: If glaze becomes too thin, add more confectioners' sugar. If glaze is too thick, add more orange juice.

Orange Cinnamon Swirl Bread

Luscious Cakes

No need to wait for a birthday or party—make any day a celebration with these fabulous cakes.

Campbell's® Tomato Soup Spice Cake

   1 package (about 18 ounces) spice cake mix
   1 can (10¾ ounces) CAMPBELL'S® Condensed Tomato Soup
½ cup water
   2 eggs
      Cream Cheese Frosting (recipe follows)

1. Preheat oven to 350°F. Grease and lightly flour two 8- or 9-inch round cake pans.

2. In large bowl mix cake mix, soup, water and eggs according to package directions.

3. Pour into prepared pans. Bake 25 minutes or until toothpick inserted in center comes out clean.

4. Cool on wire racks 10 minutes. Remove from pans and cool completely on wire racks.

5. Fill and frost with Cream Cheese Frosting.   *Makes 12 servings*

Cream Cheese Frosting: Beat 2 packages (3 ounces **each**) softened cream cheese until smooth. Gradually blend in 1 package (1 pound) sifted confectioners' sugar and ½ teaspoon vanilla extract. If desired, thin with milk.

Prep Time: 10 minutes
Bake Time: 35 minutes

Easy Carrot Cake

$^1/_2$ cup Prune Purée (recipe follows)
2 cups all-purpose flour
2 teaspoons ground cinnamon
1 $^1/_2$ teaspoons baking soda
$^1/_2$ teaspoon salt
4 cups shredded DOLE® Carrots
2 cups sugar
$^1/_2$ cup DOLE® Pineapple Juice
2 eggs
2 teaspoons vanilla extract
Vegetable cooking spray

• Prepare Prune Purée; set aside.

• Combine flour, cinnamon, baking soda and salt in medium bowl; set aside.

• Beat together Prune Purée, carrots, sugar, juice, eggs and vanilla in large bowl until blended. Add flour mixture; stir until well blended.

• Spread batter into 13×9-inch baking dish sprayed with vegetable cooking spray.

• Bake at 375°F 30 to 35 minutes or until toothpick inserted in center comes out clean. Cool completely in dish on wire rack. Dust with powdered sugar and garnish with carrot curls, if desired.

Makes 12 servings

Prune Purée: Combine 1⅓ cups DOLE® Pitted Prunes, halved, and ½ cup hot water in food processor or blender container. Process until prunes are finely chopped, stopping to scrape down sides occasionally. (Purée can be refrigerated in airtight container for up to 1 week.)

Prep Time: 15 minutes
Bake Time: 35 minutes

Easy Carrot Cake

Berry Bundt Cake

2 cups all-purpose flour
1 tablespoon baking powder
1 teaspoon baking soda
$1/4$ teaspoon salt
1 cup sugar
$3/4$ cup buttermilk
$1/2$ cup cholesterol-free egg substitute
$1/4$ cup vegetable oil
2 cups frozen unsweetened raspberries
2 cups frozen unsweetened blueberries

1. Preheat oven to 350°F. Spray 6-cup Bundt pan with nonstick cooking spray. Set aside.

2. Combine flour, baking powder, baking soda and salt in large bowl. Combine sugar, buttermilk, egg substitute and oil in medium bowl. Add sugar mixture to flour mixture; stir just until moistened.

3. Fold in raspberries and blueberries. Pour batter into prepared pan. Bake 1 hour or until wooden pick inserted in center comes out clean. Cool in pan on wire rack. Serve with fresh berries, if desired.

Makes 12 servings

Don't thaw frozen berries before adding them to batter unless the recipe directs you otherwise. Thawed berries will "bleed," leaving colored streaks in the finished baked good.

Berry Bundt Cake

Mocha Marble Pound Cake

2 cups all-purpose flour

2 teaspoons baking powder

1 teaspoon baking soda

$^1/_2$ teaspoon salt

1 cup sugar

$^1/_4$ cup FLEISCHMANN'S® Original Margarine, softened

1 teaspoon vanilla extract

$^1/_2$ cup EGG BEATERS® Healthy Real Egg Product

1 (8-ounce) container low-fat coffee yogurt

$^1/_4$ cup unsweetened cocoa

Mocha Yogurt Glaze (recipe follows)

In small bowl, combine flour, baking powder, baking soda and salt; set aside.

In large bowl, with electric mixer at medium speed, beat sugar, margarine and vanilla until creamy. Add Egg Beaters®; beat until smooth. With mixer at low speed, add yogurt alternately with flour mixture, beating well after each addition. Remove half of batter to medium bowl. Add cocoa to batter remaining in large bowl; beat until blended. Alternately spoon coffee and chocolate batters into greased 9×5×3-inch loaf pan. With knife, cut through batters to create marbled effect.

Bake at 325°F for 60 to 65 minutes or until toothpick inserted in center comes out clean. Cool in pan on wire rack for 10 minutes. Remove from pan; cool completely on wire rack. Frost with Mocha Yogurt Glaze.

Makes 16 servings

Mocha Yogurt Glaze: In small bowl, combine ½ cup powdered sugar, 1 tablespoon unsweetened cocoa and 1 tablespoon low-fat coffee yogurt until smooth; add more yogurt, if necessary, to make spreading consistency.

Prep Time: 20 minutes
Bake Time: 65 minutes

Mocha Marble Pound Cake

Mom's Favorite White Cake

2 1/4 cups cake flour

1 tablespoon baking powder

1/2 teaspoon salt

1/2 cup butter, softened

1 1/2 cups sugar

4 egg whites

2 teaspoons vanilla

1 cup milk

Strawberry Frosting (recipe follows)

Fruit Filling (recipe follows)

Fresh strawberries (optional)

Preheat oven to 350°F. Line bottoms of two 9-inch round cake pans with waxed paper; lightly grease paper. Combine flour, baking powder and salt in medium bowl; set aside.

Beat butter and sugar in large bowl with electric mixer at medium speed until light and fluffy. Add egg whites, two at a time, beating well after each addition. Add vanilla; beat until blended. With electric mixer at low speed, add flour mixture alternately with milk, beating well after each addition. Pour batter evenly into prepared pans.

Bake 25 minutes or until toothpick inserted into centers comes out clean. Cool layers in pans on wire rack 10 minutes. Loosen edges and invert layers onto rack to cool completely.

Prepare Strawberry Frosting and Fruit Filling. To fill and frost cake, place one layer on cake plate; spread top with Fruit Filling. Place second layer over filling. Frost top and sides with Strawberry Frosting. Place strawberries on top of cake, if desired. Refrigerate; allow cake to stand at room temperature 15 minutes before serving.   *Makes 12 servings*

Strawberry Frosting

2 envelopes (1.3 ounces each) whipped topping mix
$^2/_3$ cup milk
1 cup (6 ounces) white chocolate chips, melted
$^1/_4$ cup strawberry jam

Beat whipped topping mix and milk in medium bowl with electric mixer on low speed until blended. Beat on high speed 4 minutes or until topping thickens and forms peaks. With mixer at low speed, beat melted chocolate into topping. Add jam; beat until blended. Chill 15 minutes or until spreading consistency.

Fruit Filling

1 cup Strawberry Frosting (recipe above)
1 can (8 ounces) crushed pineapple, drained
1 cup sliced strawberries

Combine Strawberry Frosting, pineapple and strawberries in medium bowl; mix well.

*To keep the serving plate clean when frosting
a cake, place strips of waxed paper under the cake's
edge after positioning the cake on the plate.
Frost cake as directed. Carefully pull waxed paper
strips from under cake.*

Lemon Poppy Seed Cupcakes

CUPCAKES

  1 package DUNCAN HINES® Moist Deluxe Lemon Supreme
    Cake Mix
  3 eggs
  1 1/3 cups water
  1/3 cup vegetable oil
  3 tablespoons poppy seed

LEMON FROSTING

  1 container (16 ounces) DUNCAN HINES® Creamy Homestyle
    Vanilla Frosting
  1 teaspoon grated lemon peel
  1/4 teaspoon lemon extract
  3 to 4 drops yellow food coloring
    Yellow and orange gumdrops, for garnish

1. Preheat oven to 350°F. Place 30 (2 1/2-inch) paper liners in muffin
cups.

2. **For cupcakes,** combine cake mix, eggs, water, oil and poppy seed in
large bowl. Beat at medium speed of electric mixer 2 minutes. Fill paper
liners about half full. Bake 18 to 21 minutes or until toothpick inserted
in center comes out clean. Cool in pans 5 minutes. Remove to cooling
racks. Cool completely.

3. **For lemon frosting,** combine Vanilla frosting, lemon peel and lemon
extract in small bowl. Tint with yellow food coloring to desired color.
Frost cupcakes with lemon frosting. Decorate with gumdrops.

Makes 30 cupcakes

Lemon Poppy Seed Cupcakes

Rich Chocolate Mini-Cakes

$2/3$ cup all-purpose flour

$1/2$ cup sugar

3 tablespoons HERSHEY'S Cocoa

$1/2$ teaspoon baking powder

$1/4$ teaspoon baking soda

$1/4$ teaspoon salt

$1/2$ cup water

3 tablespoons vegetable oil

1 teaspoon vanilla extract

Chocolate Glaze (recipe follows)

Vanilla Drizzle (recipe follows)

Heat oven to 350°F. Lightly grease 24 small muffin cups ($1^{3}/4$ inches in diameter).

Stir together flour, sugar, cocoa, baking powder, baking soda and salt in medium bowl. Add water, oil and vanilla; stir or whisk until batter is smooth and blended. (Batter will be thin.) Spoon batter into prepared cups, filling $2/3$ full.

Bake 12 to 14 minutes or until top springs back when touched lightly in center. Cool in pans on wire racks 3 minutes; invert onto racks. Cool completely.

Prepare Chocolate Glaze; dip rounded portion into glaze or spread glaze on tops. Place on waxed paper-covered tray; refrigerate 10 minutes to set glaze. Prepare Vanilla Drizzle; drizzle onto mini-cakes. Decorate as desired.   *Makes about 2 dozen mini-cakes*

Chocolate Glaze: In small saucepan over low heat, melt 2 tablespoons butter or margarine; add 2 tablespoons HERSHEY'S Cocoa and 2 tablespoons water. Cook and stir until smooth and slightly thickened; *do not boil.* Remove from heat; cool slightly. Gradually blend in 1 cup powdered sugar and 1/2 teaspoon vanilla extract; beat with wire whisk until smooth and slightly thickened.

Vanilla Drizzle: In small microwave-safe bowl, microwave 1/2 cup HERSHEY'S Premier White Chips and 1 tablespoon shortening at HIGH (100% power) 30 seconds; stir until smooth. If necessary, microwave at HIGH additional 15 seconds or just until chips are melted and smooth when stirred.

Rich Chocolate Mini-Cakes

I Think You're "Marbleous" Cupcakes

1 box (18^1/$_2$ ounces) pudding-in-the-mix cake mix, any flavor

3 large eggs

^{1}/$_4$ cup oil

1 can (16 ounces) vanilla frosting

1 tube (4^1/$_4$ ounces) red decorating icing

SUPPLIES

Decorating tips to fit tube of icing

1. Preheat oven to 350°F. Grease or paper-line 24 (2^1/$_2$-inch) muffin cups.

2. Prepare cake mix according to package directions with water, eggs and oil. Spoon batter into prepared pans, filling each ^{2}/$_3$ full.

3. Bake 20 to 25 minutes or until toothpick inserted into centers comes out clean. Cool in pans 20 minutes. Remove to wire rack and cool completely.

4. Spread 1^1/$_2$ to 2 tablespoons frosting over each cupcake. Fit round tip onto tube of icing. Squeeze 4 to 5 dots icing over each cupcake. Swirl toothpick through icing and frosting in continuous motion to make marbleized pattern or heart shapes.   *Makes about 2 dozen cupcakes*

To easily transport decorated cupcakes, just put them back into the muffin pans for the trip. No more sliding or tipping!

I Think You're "Marbleous" Cupcakes

Rich & Gooey Apple-Caramel Cake

CAKE

WESSON® No-Stick Cooking Spray

2 cups all-purpose flour

1 teaspoon salt

1 teaspoon baking soda

1 teaspoon pumpkin pie spice

1 1/2 cups granulated sugar

3/4 cup WESSON® Vegetable Oil

3 eggs

2 teaspoons vanilla

3 cups peeled, cored and sliced tart apples, such as Granny Smith
(1/2-inch slices)

1 cup chopped walnuts

GLAZE

1 cup firmly packed light brown sugar

1/2 cup (1 stick) butter

1/4 cup milk

Whipped cream

For cake, preheat oven to 350°F. Spray a 13×9×2-inch baking pan with Wesson® Cooking Spray; set aside. In medium bowl, combine flour, salt, baking soda and pie spice; mix well. Set aside. In large bowl, with electric mixer, beat granulated sugar, Wesson® Oil, eggs and vanilla for 3 minutes at medium speed. Add flour mixture and stir until dry ingredients are moistened; fold in apples and walnuts. Pour batter into baking pan and spread evenly; bake 50 to 55 minutes or until wooden pick inserted into center comes out clean. Cool cake in pan on wire rack.

Meanwhile, for glaze, in small saucepan over medium heat, bring brown sugar, butter and milk to a boil, stirring until sugar has dissolved. Boil 1 minute. Spoon half of glaze over warm cake; set *remaining* aside. Allow cake to stand 5 minutes. Top *each* serving with *remaining* glaze and whipped cream.   *Makes 12 to 15 servings*

Rich & Gooey Apple-Caramel Cake

Butter Pecan Banana Cake

CAKE

    1 package DUNCAN HINES® Moist Deluxe Butter Recipe
       Golden Cake Mix

    4 eggs

    1 cup mashed ripe bananas (about 3 medium)

    ¾ cup vegetable oil

    ½ cup granulated sugar

    ¼ cup milk

    1 teaspoon vanilla extract

    1 cup chopped pecans

FROSTING

    1 cup coarsely chopped pecans

    ¼ cup butter or margarine

    1 container DUNCAN HINES® Vanilla Frosting

Preheat oven to 325°F. Grease and flour 10-inch Bundt or tube pan.

Combine cake mix, eggs, bananas, oil, sugar, milk and vanilla extract in large mixing bowl. Beat at low speed with electric mixer until moistened. Beat at medium speed for 2 minutes. Stir in 1 cup chopped pecans. Pour into prepared pan. Bake 50 to 60 minutes or until toothpick inserted in center comes out clean. Cool in pan 25 minutes. Invert onto cooling rack. Cool completely.

Place 1 cup coarsely chopped pecans and butter in skillet. Cook on medium heat, stirring until pecans are toasted. Combine nut mixture and frosting in small bowl. Cool until spreading consistency. Frost cake.

Makes 12 to 16 servings

Butter Pecan Banana Cake

Fall Harvest Spice Cake

1 package (18$^{1}/_{4}$ ounces) spice or carrot cake mix

1 cup water

3 eggs

$^{1}/_{3}$ cup vegetable oil

$^{1}/_{3}$ cup apple butter

   Maple Buttercream Frosting (recipe follows)

2 cups coarsely chopped walnuts

$^{1}/_{4}$ cup semisweet chocolate chips, melted

$^{1}/_{4}$ cup chopped almonds

2 tablespoons chopped dried apricots

2 tablespoons chopped dried cranberries

2 tablespoons raisins

1. Preheat oven to 375°F. Grease and flour two 9-inch round baking pans.

2. Combine cake mix, water, eggs, oil and apple butter in medium bowl. Beat at low speed of electric mixer until blended; beat at medium speed 2 minutes. Pour batter into prepared pans.

3. Bake 35 to 40 minutes or until toothpick inserted into centers comes out clean. Let cool in pans on wire rack 10 minutes. Remove to racks; cool completely.

4. Prepare Maple Buttercream Frosting.

5. Place 1 cake layer on serving plate; frost top with Maple Buttercream Frosting. Top with second cake layer; frost top and sides with frosting. Press walnuts onto side of cake.

6. Pipe chocolate onto cake for tree trunk. Combine almonds, apricots, cranberries and raisins. Sprinkle above and below trunk to make leaves.

Makes 12 servings

Piping Chocolate: Place chocolate chips in a resealable plastic sandwich bag. Close bag tightly. Microwave on HIGH about 45 seconds; knead chocolate until melted. Repeat if necessary, microwaving 30 seconds at a time. Twist the top of the bag tightly against the chocolate. Snip a tiny tip (about $1/8$ inch) off one corner of the bag. Hold the top of the bag tightly and pipe the chocolate through the opening.

Maple Buttercream Frosting

4 tablespoons butter or margarine, softened
$1/4$ cup maple or pancake syrup
3 cups powdered sugar

In small bowl, beat butter and syrup until blended. Gradually beat in sugar until smooth. *Makes about 3 cups*

Fall Harvest Spice Cake

Blue-Ribbon Pies

Nothing says home cooking quite like pies. The chunky fruit, crunchy nut and silky cream fillings of these pies will make mouths water and hearts long for home.

Mixed Berry Pie

9-inch Classic Crisco® Double Crust (page 119)
2 cups canned or frozen blackberries, thawed and well drained
1¹/₂ cups canned or frozen blueberries, thawed and well drained
¹/₂ cup canned or frozen gooseberries, thawed and well drained
¹/₈ teaspoon almond extract
¹/₄ cup sugar
3 tablespoons cornstarch

1. Prepare 9-inch Classic Crisco® Double Crust; press bottom crust into 9-inch pie plate. *Do not bake.* Heat oven to 425°F.

2. For filling, combine blackberries, blueberries, gooseberries and almond extract in large bowl. Combine sugar and cornstarch. Add to berries. Toss well to mix. Spoon into unbaked pie crust.

3. Cut top crust into leaf shapes and arrange on top of pie, or cover pie with top crust. Flute edge. Cut slits into top crust, if using, to allow steam to escape.

4. Bake at 425°F for 40 minutes or until filling in center is bubbly and crust is golden brown. *Do not overbake.* Cool until barely warm or at room temperature before serving. *Makes 1 (9-inch) pie*

Hershey's Cocoa Cream Pie

1 baked (9-inch) pie crust or graham cracker crumb crust, cooled
$^1/_2$ cup HERSHEY'S Cocoa
1$^1/_4$ cups sugar
$^1/_3$ cup cornstarch
$^1/_4$ teaspoon salt
3 cups milk
3 tablespoons butter or margarine
1$^1/_2$ teaspoons vanilla extract

1. Prepare crust. Stir together cocoa, sugar, cornstarch and salt in medium saucepan. Gradually add milk, stirring until smooth. Cook over medium heat, stirring constantly, until mixture comes to a boil; boil 1 minute. Remove from heat; stir in butter and vanilla.

2. Pour into prepared crust. Press plastic wrap directly onto surface. Cool to room temperature. Refrigerate 6 to 8 hours. Garnish as desired. Cover; refrigerate leftover pie. *Makes 6 to 8 servings*

Blueberry Crumble Pie

1 KEEBLER® Ready Crust® Graham Cracker Pie Crust
1 egg yolk, beaten
1 (21-ounce) can blueberry pie filling
$^1/_3$ cup all-purpose flour
$^1/_3$ cup quick-cooking oats
$^1/_4$ cup sugar
3 tablespoons margarine, melted

Preheat oven to 375°F. Brush bottom and sides of crust with egg yolk; bake on baking sheet until light brown, about 5 minutes.

Pour blueberry pie filling into crust. In small bowl, combine flour, oats and sugar; mix in melted margarine. Spoon over pie filling.

Bake on baking sheet about 35 minutes or until filling is bubbly and topping is browned.

Makes 1 pie

Prep Time: 15 minutes
Bake Time: 40 minutes

Blueberry Crumble Pie

Praline Pie

    1 (9-inch) HONEY MAID® Honey Graham Pie Crust

    1 egg white, slightly beaten

1/4 cup margarine or butter, melted

    1 cup firmly packed light brown sugar

3/4 cup all-purpose flour

    1 egg

    1 teaspoon DAVIS® Baking Powder

    1 teaspoon vanilla extract

    1 cup PLANTERS® Pecans, coarsely chopped

    Prepared whipped topping, for garnish

Preheat oven to 375°F. Brush pie crust with egg white. Bake at 375°F for 5 minutes; set aside. *Decrease oven temperature to 350°F.*

In medium bowl, with electric mixer at low speed, beat margarine or butter and brown sugar until blended. Mix in flour, egg, baking powder and vanilla until well combined. Stir in 3/4 cup pecans. Spread into prepared crust; sprinkle top with remaining 1/4 cup pecans. Bake at 350°F for 25 to 30 minutes or until lightly browned and filling is set. Cool completely on wire rack. Garnish with whipped topping.   *Makes 6 servings*

Brushing the pie crust with egg white before baking it "seals" the crust, preventing sogginess due to moisture from the filling.

Praline Pie

113

The Best Cherry Pie

Reduced-Fat Pie Pastry (recipe follows)
2 bags (12 ounces each) frozen no-sugar-added cherries, thawed
    and well drained
³/₄ cup plus 2 teaspoons sugar, divided
1 tablespoon plus 1¹/₂ teaspoons cornstarch
1 tablespoon plus 1¹/₂ teaspoons quick-cooking tapioca
1 teaspoon fat-free (skim) milk

1. Preheat oven to 425°F.

2. Roll ²/₃ of pie pastry on lightly floured surface to 9¹/₂-inch circle.
Gently press pastry into 8-inch pie pan.

3. Combine cherries, ³/₄ cup sugar, cornstarch and tapioca in large bowl.
Spoon cherry mixture into pastry. Roll remaining pastry into circle large
enough to fit top of pie; trim off any excess pastry. Cover pie with crust. Press
edges of top and bottom crust together; trim and flute. Cut steam vents in top
of pie; brush with milk and sprinkle with remaining 2 teaspoons sugar.

4. Bake 10 minutes. Reduce heat to 375°F; bake 45 to 50 minutes or
until pie is bubbly and crust is golden. (Cover edge of crust with foil, if
necessary, to prevent burning.) Cool on wire rack; serve warm.

Makes 8 servings

Reduced-Fat Pie Pastry

2 cups all-purpose flour
2 tablespoons sugar
¹/₂ teaspoon baking powder
¹/₄ teaspoon salt
7 tablespoons cold shortening
6 to 8 tablespoons ice water, divided

1. Combine flour, sugar, baking powder and salt in medium bowl. Cut in shortening with pastry blender or 2 knives until mixture resembles coarse crumbs. Mix in water, 1 tablespoon at a time, until stiff dough is formed.

2. Cover dough with plastic wrap; refrigerate 30 minutes.

Makes 1 (8-inch) double crust

Cook's Tip: When rolling out pastry for crust, repair any tears by moistening the edges with water and using small pieces of the trimmings to patch the tears.

The Best Cherry Pie

Texas Chocolate Peanut Butter Pie

CRUST

$1^1/2$ cups graham cracker crumbs

$^1/2$ cup sugar

$^1/2$ cup (1 stick) butter, melted

FILLING

16 ounces cream cheese, at room temperature

2 cups creamy peanut butter

$1^3/4$ cups sugar

1 cup heavy whipping cream

TOPPING

$^2/3$ cup heavy whipping cream

$^1/3$ cup sugar

3 ounces semisweet chocolate

$^1/2$ cup (1 stick) butter

1 teaspoon vanilla extract

For crust, preheat oven to 350°F. Combine graham cracker crumbs with sugar and melted butter. Stir until thoroughly blended. Press mixture into bottom and up side of 10-inch pie plate. Bake crust for 10 minutes; set aside to cool.

For filling, mix cream cheese, peanut butter and $1^3/4$ cups sugar in medium bowl until blended. Whip 1 cup heavy cream until stiff, then fold into cream cheese mixture. Spoon filling into cooled crust.

For topping, combine ⅔ cup heavy cream and ⅓ cup sugar in saucepan and bring to a boil. Reduce heat and simmer for 7 minutes. Remove pan from heat. Add chocolate and butter; stir until melted. Stir in vanilla. Cool until slightly thickened. Pour evenly over pie. Refrigerate 4 to 5 hours before serving. Garnish with toasted peanuts.

Makes one 10-inch pie (8 to 10 servings)

Favorite recipe from **Texas Peanut Producers Board**

Texas Chocolate Peanut Butter Pie

Sumptuous Strawberry Rhubarb Pie

CRUST

 9-inch Classic Crisco® Double Crust (recipe follows)

FILLING

 4 cups fresh cut rhubarb ($^1/_2$-inch pieces)

 3 cups sliced strawberries

 1$^1/_3$ cups sugar

 $^1/_3$ cup plus $^1/_4$ cup all-purpose flour

 2 tablespoons plus 1$^1/_2$ teaspoons quick-cooking tapioca

 $^1/_2$ teaspoon grated orange peel

 $^1/_2$ teaspoon ground cinnamon

 $^1/_4$ teaspoon ground nutmeg

 2 tablespoons butter or margarine

GLAZE

 1 egg, beaten

 1 tablespoon sugar

1. Prepare 9-inch Classic Crisco® Double Crust; roll and press bottom crust into 9-inch pie plate. *Do not bake.* Heat oven to 425°F.

2. For Filling, combine rhubarb and strawberries in large bowl. Combine 1$^1/_3$ cups sugar, flour, tapioca, orange peel, cinnamon and nutmeg in medium bowl; stir well. Add to fruit. Toss to coat. Spoon filling into unbaked pie crust. Dot with butter. Moisten pastry edge with water.

3. Roll out top crust. Lift onto filled pie. Trim $^1/_2$ inch beyond edge of pie plate. Fold top edge under bottom crust; flute. Cut desired shapes into top crust to allow steam to escape.

4. For Glaze, brush top crust with egg. Sprinkle with 1 tablespoon sugar.

5. Bake at 425°F for 40 to 50 minutes or until filling in center is bubbly and crust is golden brown. *Do not overbake.* Cover edge with foil, if necessary, to prevent overbrowning. Cool until barely warm or at room temperature before serving.

Makes 1 (9-inch) pie

9-inch Classic Crisco® Double Crust

    2 cups all-purpose flour
    1 teaspoon salt
    ¾ CRISCO® Stick or ¾ cup CRISCO® all-vegetable shortening
    5 tablespoons cold water

1. Spoon flour into measuring cup and level. Combine flour and salt in medium bowl.

2. Cut in shortening using pastry blender or 2 knives until flour is blended to form pea-size chunks.

3. Sprinkle with water, 1 tablespoon at a time. Toss lightly with fork until dough forms a ball.

4. Divide dough in half. Press half of dough between hands to form a 5- to 6-inch "pancake." Flour rolling surface and rolling pin lightly. Roll dough into circle. Trim circle 1 inch larger than upside-down pie plate. Carefully remove trimmed dough. Set aside to reroll and use for pastry cutout garnish, if desired. Repeat with remaining half of dough.

Makes 2 (9-inch) crusts

Fruit Tart

$^1/_3$ cup FLEISCHMANN'S® Original Margarine

1$^1/_4$ cups all-purpose flour

4 to 5 tablespoons ice water

1 cup EGG BEATERS® Healthy Real Egg Product

$^1/_3$ cup sugar

1 teaspoon vanilla extract

1$^1/_4$ cups skim milk, scalded

1 cup sliced fresh fruit

In medium bowl, cut margarine into flour until mixture resembles coarse crumbs. Add water, 1 tablespoon at a time, tossing until moistened. Shape into a ball. On floured surface, roll dough into 11-inch circle, about $^1/_8$ inch thick. Place in 9-inch pie plate, making a $^1/_2$-inch-high fluted edge; set aside.

In medium bowl, combine Egg Beaters®, sugar and vanilla; gradually stir in milk. Pour into prepared crust. Bake at 350°F for 45 to 50 minutes or until set. Cool completely on wire rack. Cover; chill until firm, about 2 hours. To serve, top with fruit.   *Makes 10 servings*

Prep Time: 30 minutes
Bake Time: 45 minutes

Scalding milk is heating the milk almost, but not quite, to the boiling point. Place 1$^1/_4$ cups of cold milk in a 2-cup microwavable glass measure. Heat at HIGH 2$^1/_2$ to 3 minutes or until milk is bubbly near edge of measure.

Fruit Tart

ACKNOWLEDGMENTS

The publisher would like to thank the companies and organizations listed below for the use of their recipes and photographs in this publication.

California Strawberry Commission

Campbell Soup Company

ConAgra Grocery Products Company

Dole Food Company, Inc.

Duncan Hines® and Moist Deluxe® are registered trademarks of Aurora Foods Inc.

Egg Beaters®

Hershey Foods Corporation

HONEY MAID® Honey Grahams

Keebler Company

Kraft Foods, Inc.

M&M/MARS

The Procter & Gamble Company

Texas Peanut Producers Board

Almonds: Fabulous
Blonde Brownies,
64
Apple
Rich & Gooey Apple-
Caramel Cake, 102
Soft Apple Cider
Cookies, 11
Apple Butter Spice
Muffins, 70
Applesauce-Spice Bread,
78

Baker's® Chocolate Chunk
Banana Bread, 80
Baker's® Chocolate Chunk
Sour Cream Muffins,
74
Baker's® One Bowl®
Brownies, 60
Bananas
Baker's® Chocolate
Chunk Banana
Bread, 80
Butter Pecan Banana
Cake, 104
Berry Bundt Cake, 90
Blackberries: Mixed Berry
Pie, 109
Blueberry
Berry Bundt Cake, 90
Blueberry Crumble Pie,
110
Mixed Berry Pie, 109
Brunch-Time Zucchini-
Date Bread, 72
Butter Pecan Banana
Cake, 104
Butterscotch Brownies,
63

Campbell's® Tomato Soup
Spice Cake, 87
Caramel Filling, 29
Caramel Fudge Brownies,
62
Cherries
Cherry Butterscotch
Bars, 45
The Best Cherry Pie,
114
Choco-Caramel Delights,
28
Chocolate
Choco-Caramel
Delights, 28
Chocolate Glaze, 99
Chocolate Orange
Gems, 38
Choco-Lowfat
Strawberry
Shortbread Bars,
32
Double "Topped"
Brownies, 52
Hershey's Cocoa Cream
Pie, 110
Marbled Biscotti,
20
Marbled Peanut Butter
Brownies, 54
Mini Brownie Cups,
56
Mocha Marble Pound
Cake, 92
Mocha Yogurt Glaze,
92
Rich Chocolate Mini-
Cakes, 98
Texas Chocolate Peanut
Butter Pie, 116

Chocolate, Baking
Baker's® Chocolate
Chunk Banana
Bread, 80
Baker's® Chocolate
Chunk Sour Cream
Muffins, 74
Baker's® One Bowl®
Brownies, 60
Caramel Fudge
Brownies, 62
Creamy Quick
Chocolate Frosting, 67
Quick & Easy Fudgey
Brownies, 66
Toffee Chunk Brownie
Cookies, 18
Chocolate Caramel Pecan
Bars, 36
Chocolate Chips
Butterscotch Brownies,
63
Chocolate Caramel
Pecan Bars, 36
Chocolate Chip Cookie
Bars, 42
Marshmallow Krispie
Bars, 48
Minted Chocolate Chip
Brownies, 58
Naomi's Revel Bars, 31
Peanut Butter Chocolate
Chippers, 22
Rocky Road Brownies,
51
Walnut-Chocolate
Quick Bread, 69
Chocolate Glaze, 99
Chocolate Orange Gems,
38

Choco-Lowfat Strawberry Shortbread Bars, 32
Cider Glaze, 11
Cranberries: Cranberry Poppy Seed Loaf, 76
Cream Cheese
Brunch-Time Zucchini-Date Bread, 72
Cream Cheese Frosting, 87
Currant Cheesecake Bars, 46
Texas Chocolate Peanut Butter Pie, 116
Creamy Quick Chocolate Frosting, 67
Cupcakes
I Think You're "Marbleous" Cupcakes, 100
Lemon Poppy Seed Cupcakes, 96
Rich Chocolate Mini-Cakes, 98
Currant Cheesecake Bars, 46

Double "Topped" Brownies, 52

Easy Carrot Cake, 88
Easy Lemon Cookies, 17

Fabulous Blonde Brownies, 64
Fall Harvest Spice Cake, 106
Frostings and Glazes
Chocolate Glaze, 99
Cider Glaze, 11

Cream Cheese Frosting, 87
Creamy Quick Chocolate Frosting, 67
Maple Buttercream Frosting, 107
Mocha Glaze, 57
Mocha Yogurt Glaze, 92
Powdered Sugar Glaze, 76
Strawberry Frosting, 95
Vanilla Glaze, 39
White Chocolate Glaze, 60
Fruit Filling, 95
Fruit Tart, 120

Gingerbread Pear Muffins, 81

Hershey's Cocoa Cream Pie, 110
Honey Ginger Snaps, 14

I Think You're "Marbleous" Cupcakes, 100

Lemon
Lemon Poppy Seed Cupcakes, 96
Luscious Lemon Bars, 34
Luscious Lemon Bars, 34

Maple Buttercream Frosting, 107
Marbled Biscotti, 20
Marbled Peanut Butter Brownies, 54

Marshmallows
Marshmallow Krispie Bars, 48
Rocky Road Brownies, 51
Mexican Wedding Cookies, 16
Mini Brownie Cups, 56
Minted Chocolate Chip Brownies, 58
Mixed Berry Pie, 109
Mocha Glaze, 57
Mocha Marble Pound Cake, 92
Mocha Yogurt Glaze, 92
Mom's Favorite White Cake, 94
Muffins
Apple Butter Spice Muffins, 70
Baker's® Chocolate Chunk Sour Cream Muffins, 74
Gingerbread Pear Muffins, 81
Nutmeg Strawberry Muffins, 82
Mystical Layered Bars, 48

Naomi's Revel Bars, 31
9-Inch Classic Crisco® Double Crust, 119
Nutmeg Strawberry Muffins, 82
Nuts (see also individual nuts)
Baker's® One Bowl® Brownies, 60
Quick & Easy Fudgey Brownies, 66

Oats
Naomi's Revel Bars, 31
Oatmeal Raisin
    Cookies, 27
Strawberry Oat Bars,
    40
Orange Cinnamon Swirl
    Bread, 84

Peanut Butter
Marbled Peanut Butter
    Brownies, 54
Marshmallow Krispie
    Bars, 48
Peanut Butter
    Chocolate Chippers,
    22
Texas Chocolate Peanut
    Butter Pie, 116
Peanuts: Peanut Gems, 26
Pecans
Butter Pecan Banana
    Cake, 104
Choco-Caramel
    Delights, 28
Chocolate Caramel
    Pecan Bars, 36
Chocolate Chip Cookie
    Bars, 42
Chocolate Orange
    Gems, 38
Easy Lemon Cookies,
    17
Mexican Wedding
    Cookies, 16
Mystical Layered Bars,
    48
Pecan Pie Bars, 44
Praline Pie, 112
Powdered Sugar Glaze, 76

Praline Pie, 112
Prune Purée, 89

Quick & Easy Fudgey
    Brownies, 66
Quick Breads
Applesauce-Spice
    Bread, 78
Baker's® Chocolate
    Chunk Banana
    Bread, 80
Brunch-Time Zucchini-
    Date Bread, 72
Cranberry Poppy Seed
    Loaf, 76
Orange Cinnamon
    Swirl Bread, 84
Walnut-Chocolate
    Quick Bread, 69

Raspberries: Berry Bundt
    Cake, 90
Reduced-Fat Pie Pastry,
    114
Refrigerator Cookies,
    24
Rich & Gooey Apple-
    Caramel Cake, 102
Rich Chocolate Mini-
    Cakes, 98
Rocky Road Brownies, 51

Soft Apple Cider Cookies,
    11
Strawberry
Choco-Lowfat
    Strawberry
    Shortbread Bars,
    32
Fruit Filling, 95

Mom's Favorite White
    Cake, 94
Nutmeg Strawberry
    Muffins, 82
Strawberry Frosting, 95
Strawberry Oat Bars, 40
Sumptuous Strawberry
    Rhubarb Pie, 118
Sumptuous Strawberry
    Rhubarb Pie, 118

Texas Chocolate Peanut
    Butter Pie, 116
The Best Cherry Pie,
    114
Toffee Chunk Brownie
    Cookies, 18

Vanilla Drizzle, 99
Vanilla Glaze, 39

Walnuts
Fall Harvest Spice Cake,
    106
Nutmeg Strawberry
    Muffins, 82
Rich & Gooey Apple-
    Caramel Cake, 102
Rocky Road Brownies,
    51
Walnut-Chocolate
    Quick Bread, 69
White Chip Drizzle, 33
White Chocolate
Fabulous Blonde
    Brownies, 64
Fruit Filling, 95
White Chip Drizzle, 33
White Chocolate Glaze,
    60

VOLUME MEASUREMENTS (dry)

1/8 teaspoon = 0.5 mL
1/4 teaspoon = 1 mL
1/2 teaspoon = 2 mL
3/4 teaspoon = 4 mL
1 teaspoon = 5 mL
1 tablespoon = 15 mL
2 tablespoons = 30 mL
1/4 cup = 60 mL
1/3 cup = 75 mL
1/2 cup = 125 mL
2/3 cup = 150 mL
3/4 cup = 175 mL
1 cup = 250 mL
2 cups = 1 pint = 500 mL
3 cups = 750 mL
4 cups = 1 quart = 1 L

VOLUME MEASUREMENTS (fluid)

1 fluid ounce (2 tablespoons) = 30 mL
4 fluid ounces (1/2 cup) = 125 mL
8 fluid ounces (1 cup) = 250 mL
12 fluid ounces (1 1/2 cups) = 375 mL
16 fluid ounces (2 cups) = 500 mL

WEIGHTS (mass)

1/2 ounce = 15 g
1 ounce = 30 g
3 ounces = 90 g
4 ounces = 120 g
8 ounces = 225 g
10 ounces = 285 g
12 ounces = 360 g
16 ounces = 1 pound = 450 g

DIMENSIONS

1/16 inch = 2 mm
1/8 inch = 3 mm
1/4 inch = 6 mm
1/2 inch = 1.5 cm
3/4 inch = 2 cm
1 inch = 2.5 cm

OVEN TEMPERATURES

250°F = 120°C
275°F = 140°C
300°F = 150°C
325°F = 160°C
350°F = 180°C
375°F = 190°C
400°F = 200°C
425°F = 220°C
450°F = 230°C

BAKING PAN SIZES

Utensil	Size in Inches/Quarts	Metric Volume	Size in Centimeters
Baking or Cake Pan (square or rectangular)	8×8×2	2 L	20×20×5
	9×9×2	2.5 L	23×23×5
	12×8×2	3 L	30×20×5
	13×9×2	3.5 L	33×23×5
Loaf Pan	8×4×3	1.5 L	20×10×7
	9×5×3	2 L	23×13×7
Round Layer Cake Pan	8×1½	1.2 L	20×4
	9×1½	1.5 L	23×4
Pie Plate	8×1¼	750 mL	20×3
	9×1¼	1 L	23×3
Baking Dish or Casserole	1 quart	1 L	—
	1½ quart	1.5 L	—
	2 quart	2 L	—